METRICAL PASTIMES.

FOUNTAIN ROCK.

Alan Simpson.

FOUNTAIN ROCK,

AMY WIER,

AND

OTHER METRICAL PASTIMES.

BY

GEORGE HAY RINGGOLD,

U. S. A.

"What shadows we are, what shadows we pursue!"

NEW YORK:
W. A. TOWNSEND AND COMPANY.
1860.

C. A. ALVORD, STEREOTYPER AND PRINTER, 15 VANDEWATER STREET, N. Y.

CONTENTS.

To My Children.

I.

FOUNTAIN ROCK.

FOUNTAIN ROCK.

INVOCATION TO MEMORY.

"Artist rare! whose pencil brings
To view the forms of perished things;
Whose faithful, yet whose sadd'ning touch,
Of the sweet past portrays so much;
And with the tints thy pallet bears—
Those sombre hues of vanished years—
While warm the bright'ning picture glows,
O'er all a pensive shadow throws:
Thee I invoke! whose wondrous art
So captivates the wounded heart,
That in thy mirror, for each grief,
Reflected lies some sweet relief,
A little while the soul to bless,
And cheat it of its bitterness.

Thy power alone can fill my gaze
With visions of departed days;
Alone can thy unrivaled skill
With long-lost joys the canvas fill.
Thy task begin then, graphic maid,
With spirit let the sketch be made;
Shades of vanished times renew,
Paint the picture strong and true;
And while before my eager eye
The panorama passes by,
And each sweet scene, with softened ray,
One moment glows, then glides away,
Pause whene'er that hallowed place,
My childhood's happy home, I trace.
And grant, O generous Nymph, one boon—
Let me detain the bright cartoon,
Whose faithful outline fills my brain
With thee, old Fountain Rock, again.
And on each feature let me dwell,
Let me scan each object well,
Each op'ning flower, each tender leaf,
With beauty tinted—bright, but brief.
Then let some glow of generous fire
With truth and force my song inspire,

And in gay measures flowing fast,
Call up the spirit of the past."

I.

Dearest of all the spots of earth,
That sweetly smiled upon my birth,
Where first the vital air I drew,
Invigorate with wholesome dew,
Where calmly slept the unfathomed sea
Of my unconscious infancy,
And 'mid bright birds and budding flowers,
Flew childhood's sweet and rosy hours;
Methinks e'en now, in summer bloom,
I see thee in the distance loom,
As winding down the shady road,
I reach the gate beside the wood.
Here let me yield to sweet delay,
Nor in my haste be drawn away,
Till every tree, or stump, or stone,
Rises, familiar, one by one.
In each some pleasing memory lives,
That silently its welcome gives,
Not framed in studied phrase of art,
But speaking sweetly to the heart.

II.

At length is neared the grassy brook,
Where oft I've sat with line and hook,
And if a tiny minnow took,
With prize so rich I felt more pride,
I ween, than half the world beside—
More pure delight than conquerors, far,
With all their laurels won in war.

III.

At every step more eager grown,
With quickening pace I hurry on,
And now I rise the hill at last;
The hedge is neared—the gate is passed—
The path with sudden turn displays,
Full bursting on my raptured gaze,
The Eden of my early days.
And oh! with what impetuous gush,
Old feelings through my bosom rush;
The same sensations thrill me through,
As when a boy they used to do.
How well I mind at that sweet time,
With youth's bright blossoms in their prime,

When absent for a single day,
I sighed the weary hours away,
And thought the moment ne'er would come,
To seek once more my own blest home.

IV.

Now, as of yore, the peaceful scene
Extends in loveliness serene;
The white-walled mansion, stretching wide
Its airy wings on either side;
The slated roof, the dormers grey,
Touched by the morning's misty ray;
The stately poplars, lifting high
Their mitred heads against the sky;
The oval plot, the road around,
That served us for our racing ground,
Where oft we strove like blooded bays,
To reach the goal and win the praise;
Yet, harmless as this sport appears,
'Tis the dark type of future years—
First print of passion's hand on life—
Baptismal mark of after strife;
For at our childhood's very dawn,
The seeds of rivalry are sown,

And emulation's germ is nursed
With fostering care, until, at first
A puny shrub, it grows to be
Ambition's deadly Upas tree.
Alas! the troubled heart of man
Throbs on through life as it began;
With youth's first flush 'tis taught to crave,
Nor finds repose but in the grave.

V.

How quiet sleeps the grassy green!
Here at the musing hour of e'en,
When cooling dews begin to fall,
'Tis sweet, beneath this old gray wall,
Where thickly weaves the mantling vine,
To mark the twilight's mild decline,
As its last ling'ring tints decay
Before the full moon's mellow ray,
That, streaming o'er yon Eastern wood,
Bathes it in a silvery flood;
While in calm ether poised above,
The lazy clouds forget to move;
And the soft hour invites the throng
Of insects to their evening song;

While all around, below, above,
Breathe such an air of peace and love,
Enchantment seems with gentle sway,
To lure the willing soul away.
But changed with manhood's serious years,
This holy, quiet scene appears;
The present hath, with altered mien,
Thrust its cold shadow in between,
And saddened down that cheerful tone,
Till sombrous now as is its own.
Yet doth the moon, with tender light,
Smile through the shadows of the night,
Bringing with her a beauty, too,
The golden sunlight never knew.
'Tis thus when life's best hours have flown,
And twilight cold comes creeping on,
We look beyond this ruined waste,
A gleam seems wid'ning in the east;
We leave our broken dreams behind,
In heaven's own light our joys to find.

VI.

And here, when noon-day warm and bright,
Had heavenward wooed the dews of night,

I loved at hide-and-seek to play,
Among the tents of new-made hay.
Again methinks I hear the sound
Of merry laughter pealing round,
From yonder troop of romping boys,
Companions of my youthful joys.
And 'tis so sweet again to trace
The features of each welcome face—
The sparkling eye—the ruddy cheek—
The lips ne'er parted but to speak
In young delight's wild, thoughtless glee
Of hope, and love, and ecstacy.
Play on, O blessed childhood, play!
No thorns beset thy flowery way;
All thy joys are born above,
And guarded by an angel's love,
Till, full matured, they wander thence,
To light on truth and innocence;
Ling'ring a little season here,
Making all things bright appear,
But when years to youth are given,
Flying back again to heaven.

VII.

At length I reach, in bright'ning mood,
The grassy knoll where oft I've stood,
And gaze o'er field, and hill, and wood;
Mark the broad vale, the mountains blue,
Distant ranging in the view;
The pleasant fields, the meadows gay
With many a rick of fragrant hay;
The hawthorn hedge with berries red,
The lawn a perfect flower-bed;
The dingle deep around the spring,
Where used the russet wren to sing,
And, with the robin and the thrush,
Made melody in every bush;
While darting through the flowers was heard
The green enameled humming-bird.
Lo! in the East the morn appears,
Glist'ning, wet with night's fresh tears;
And playfully a gentle breeze
Is murmuring through the leafy trees.
Flowers around of every hue,
Bend with the weight of morning dew;
The lark pours forth her carol blithe,

The mower sweeps his dripping scythe,
While down yon narrow lane, just seen
O'er the tall corn that waves between,
The heifers to the meadow pass,
To feed upon the juicy grass;
And quietly on yonder hill—
Around whose foot a gentle rill,
By flowery banks, with easy flow,
Goes murmuring to the meads below—
Browsing there the bleating sheep,
In timid crowds together keep,
While falls upon the pleased ear,
The shepherd's whistle, sweet and clear;
With chorus joyous, full, and free,
From the feathered minstrelsy.

VIII.

Leaving this cherished scene behind,
Along the straggling path I wind,
And soon spreads out the garden neat,
Like chaste embroidery, at my feet.
Here art and nature strive to bring,
Each one, a richer offering;
Here bright Pomona's smiles appear,

To promise plenty to the year;
And green-clad growth with noiseless tread,
Glides easy o'er each flowery bed,
Leads by the hand luxuriance wild,
Nor cares to check her wayward child;
And luscious fruits of every hue,
The blushing peach, the damson blue,
The gage, the ripe and juicy pear,
Low drooping boughs inviting bear.
And there, too, stands the rude old bower—
The cool retreat in sunny hour;
Where vines, thick woven overhead,
Throw all within in mystic shade.
Here, sheltered from the fervid noon,
That browns the brow of ruddy June,
With rested cheek I've often sate,
And mused upon my doubtful fate;
And I have thought 'twere better far,
When passion raged her frantic war,
With life still young to sound retreat,
To fly her fierce meridian heat,
And for a refuge seek to find
The bower of the tranquil mind.

IX.

Now let me to the fancy yield,
And seek the golden harvest field;
Where, reclined in pleasant shade,
By a spreading locust made,
Wooing the uncertain breeze,
That, whispering among the trees,
Full freighted comes from green retreat
With wild herbs' perfume, fresh and sweet,
As of yore, with eye serene,
I contemplate the busy scene—
The rolling slopes of ripened grain,
Like the gently swelling main,
On whose edge the sturdy troop,
To the rustling treasure stoop;
And hum of distant voices hear,
Sweetly droning on the ear;
Or the cradles' crashing sweep,
That in a measured cadence keep,
While in rear the rustic train,
Tent with yellow shocks the plain

X.

From this fair scene, where labor browned,
With plenty's golden wreath is crowned,
I half reluctant turn away,
Through other cherished haunts to stray.
But fierce the noon-tide fervor glows,
And yon oak-grove with wide spread boughs
For me a rural bower has made,
And calls me to enjoy its shade.
Here scathless from the storms of years,
A massy rock its form uprears,
Crowned with rank growth of weeds, and grass,
And vines, that in a tangled mass
Hang o'er its rough and frowning face,
Down to the cleft that rends its base;
From whose dark jaws, with constant gush,
Bright silvery streams of water rush,
And fill, with sweetly murmuring sound,
The leafy nooks that lie around.
Wearied, I reach this gelid spring,
Upon whose mossy brink, I fling
Myself at easy length, or lave
My limbs in its refreshing wave.

2

Sweet stream! how much to thee I owe!
Along thy current's gentle flow,
With all of youth's keen zest, I'd fain
Indulge in childhood's sports again;
Launch pigmy ships upon the tide,
Thy tiny waves in state to ride,
As sails that sweep the ocean wide.
Or light, from rock to rock I'd bound,
O'er gurgling runnels eddying round,
Or watch the little fish that swim
Around thy mossy margin's rim.

XI.

Sweet Fountain Rock! where'er I stray,
My heart to thee still finds its way,
Still in each cherished scene delays,
And all my favorite haunts portrays.
Child as I was, yet still to me
There was a magic witchery
In the unfrequented dell,
Where holy quiet loves to dwell,
In the dark and lonely glen,
With Meditation far from men;
Now leaving noisy Mirth behind,

O'er Autumn's sun-browned hills to wind,
Anon with fancy for my guide,
To thread the streamlet's sedgy side,
Or hold in yonder sombre wood,
A parlance sweet with solitude.

XII.

Dear spot, alas! for me no more
Shall Spring thy vernal bloom restore;
Thy Summer charms shall bud and die,
But greet no more my longing eye;
Thy Autumn's bracing breeze shall be
Surcharged with health, but not for me;
For now thy wide and smiling lands
Have passed into a stranger's hands,
And years have flown, life's brightest—best,
Since thy sweet fields my steps have pressed.
Yet though no parents kind are there,
To raise for me a pious prayer,
Or Winter evenings to employ
In thinking of their absent boy,
Nor kindred hearts impatient burn
To hail the wanderer's return;
Yet home I must regard thee still,

Though strangers now thy portals fill;
Though now, within thy saddened hall,
Strange voices speak—strange footsteps fall;
For there is home where most we find
To sooth and satisfy the mind,
Whether it in the present lie,
Or in the fields of memory.

XIII.

When life's short race shall ended be,
And naught but dust remains of me,
That mouldering dust I'd fain have laid
In thy green grave-yard's quiet shade.
And though no sculptured stone relate,
"Here sleep the ashes of the great"—
Yet flowers as fair will o'er me bloom
As ever decked a hero's tomb.
And to my humble, lowly grave—
A boast the mighty seldom have—
Oft when gray evening's dusky wing,
Its shadow o'er the spot shall fling,
Some loyal heart shall come to spend
An hour's vigils with his friend.
But not the tears of grief alone

Shall fall upon the nameless stone;
Like dews that weep at summer e'en,
Yet gem with light the lonely green,
The bitterest drops that spring from woe
Shall find some sweetness as they flow,
And hope, with joy, her close ally,
Shall glisten in the mourner's eye,
When angels seem to whisper near,
That in a better—brighter sphere,
Friends meet once more, though parted here.

II.

AMY WIER.

AMY WIER.

I.

This is the dear old spot!
So little changed, too, with these fleeting years,
Life seems a dream—a thing forgot,
With all its hopes and fears.

II.

My heart as then is stirred,
When long ago one summer evening, I
This leafy stream's low music heard,
As it went rippling by.

III.

And o'er yon fleecy pile,
As sheds the round moon now her pearly light,
Just such a heavenly radiant smile,
She gave to that sweet night.

IV.

Thus standing here again,
I fall to musing on our childhood's years,
A throng of joys for every pain!
Smiles ever chasing tears!

V.

Our childhood's years, I said,
For with my own, another image came,
That of a little brown-haired maid,
Amy, her simple name.

VI.

Life like a lake did lie,
No breath of passion stirred its waters then,
A youth of fourteen summers I,
She but a child of ten.

VII.

But as my Amy grew,
And passed from youth to thoughtful woman-
hood,
Born in my breast a passion new,
Rose like an April flood.

VIII.

Yet by no word of mine,
Or look that might a loving thought make known,
Sought I to let her heart divine
The secret of my own.

IX.

For if I e'er began,
Honor would check me with a stern reproof;
Her father was my guardian,
And I, beneath his roof.

X.

But love, like light, its track
Breaks through the cold clear ice of self-control,
Its subtile signals, darting back
And forth, from soul to soul.

XI.

And thus, whate'er might seem,
By sense refined each heart the other knew,
While silently as in a dream,
Love's golden season flew,

XII.

Till by and by, the hour
Of parting came, and I was sent away,
At learning's source to gather store,
Life's sterner part to play.

XIII.

And thus some seasons fled,
When homeward bound I found myself once
more;
While with a mingled hope and dread,
My heart was running o'er.

XIV.

At length the house I neared—
Moonlight and shadow on each angled wall—
And sounds of merry music heard,
Within the lighted hall.

XV.

Some tongues there'll always be,
With good or bad intent ill news tc bear,
And such there now were near to me,
To whisper in my ear.

XVI.

Another's name, not mine,
They told me that my Amy soon would bear,
With orange blossoms he'd entwine
My Amy's nut-brown hair.

XVII.

Stunned by the sudden blow,
That crushed the fabric hope had reared so high,
I would have given the world to know,
That moment I could die.

XVIII.

'Twas but a moment though,
And then I cast the impious thought from me;
"Teach me, my God," I cried, "to bow
My soul to thy decree."

XIX.

How wonderful the peace
That in an instant sometimes answers prayer,
Thus in my heart could not but cease,
The promptings of despair.

XX.

Yet throbbed with keenest pain,
That cruel wound, time's balm alone could heal,
For though my heart might not complain,
It could not cease to feel.

XXI.

Thus, in more tranquil mind,
I sought the brook-side sheltered by this wood,
For wounded spirits ever find
Solace in solitude.

XXII.

And sadly here I sat,
Though fresh as now the velvet verdure grew,
And seemed, all earth to saturate,
The breath of evening dew.

XXIII.

Ah! I remember well,
Death, than that day, could not more cruel be,
Whose vesper hour had tolled the knell
Of earthly joys for me.

XXIV.

Thus, then, revealed to none,
Must lie the secret of my heart's disease,
Nor dared I, save when thus alone,
To utter words like these:

XXV.

"Farewell! dear Amy Wier,
Farewell! forever art thou lost to me—
Lost, though no time can ever tear
Thee from my memory.

XXVI.

"I might have won thy love,
This night, perhaps, my bride thou might'st have been,
But where the right could not approve,
I would not wish to win."

XXVII.

The word I scarce had said,
When well-nigh froze the current of my blood,
For there her father and the maid,
All breathing near me stood.

XXVIII.

"Well done, indeed, my boy!
Right nobly done!" with warmth the old man cried,
"That gold hath surely no alloy,
By fire that's purified.

XXIX.

"Its right arm Heaven assures,
To pilot him whose course is just and true;
My daughter's heart was always yours,
So shall her hand be too.

XXX.

"While stand the heavens and earth,
In time's hand-writing shall the record live—
God's bounty can, than honest worth,
No nobler title give."

XXXI.

The rising tear repressed,
Yet might the beating of my heart be heard,
I drew my Amy to my breast,
Without a spoken word.

XXXII.

And many a day has flown,
And much of sunshine rested on my life,
For Amy she has been my own,
My joy—my hope—my wife.

XXXIII.

And blessed 'tis again,
After long years in this dear spot to be,
With heart no older grown than then,
For Amy sits by me.

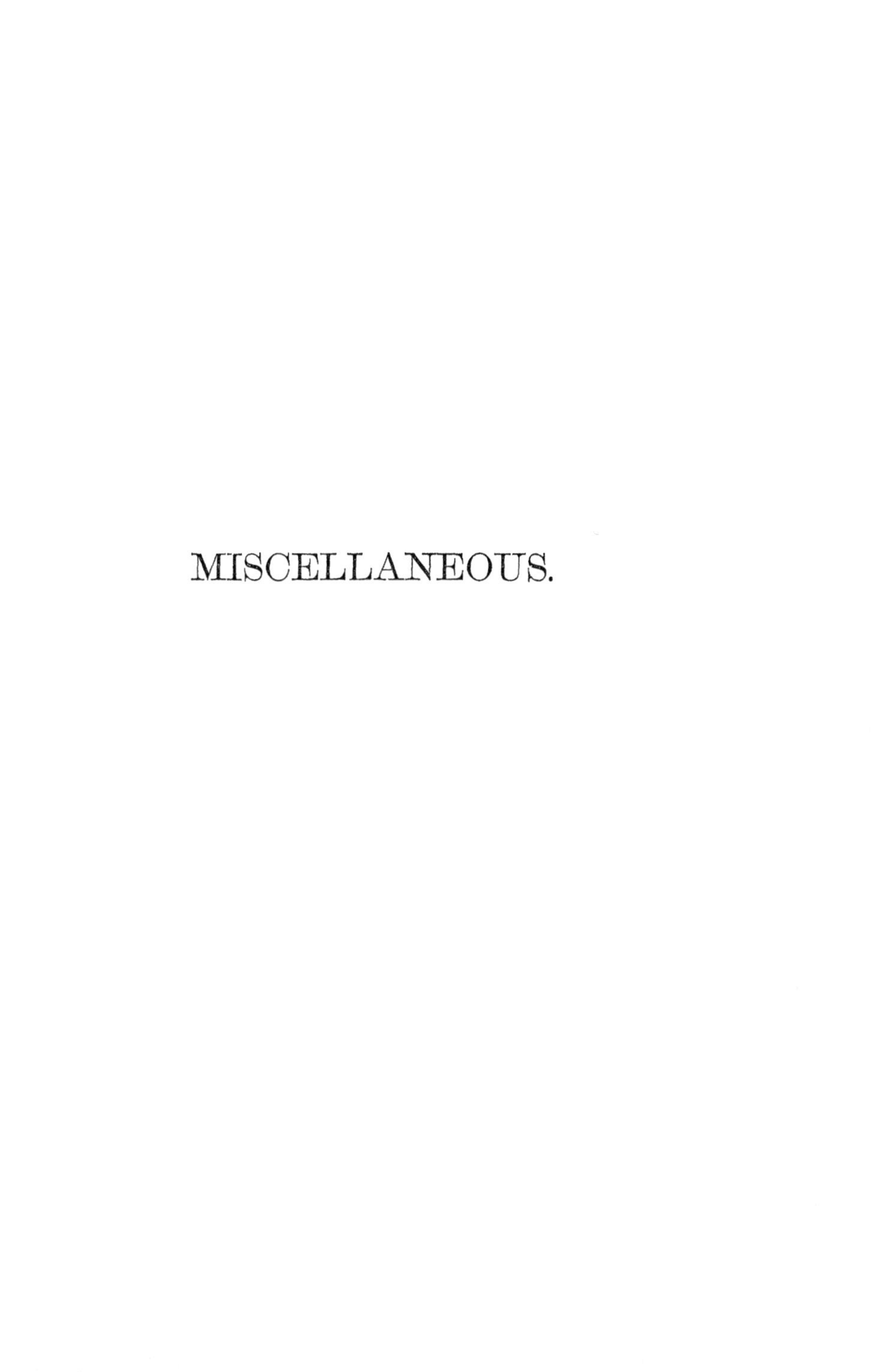

MISCELLANEOUS.

ELÖISE.

Rounded form of faultless mould,
Such, in marble chaste and cold,
Wrought the master hands of old.

O'er each temple's swelling sphere,
Casting dreamy shadows there,
Flow the tresses of her hair,

As waves their sister waves pursue;
Nor brown, nor flaxen is their hue,
But of a shade between the two.

Deeply blue as Tuscan skies,
Are her quiet, thoughtful eyes—
Orbs like Eve's in Paradise.

Fresh her cheek, but coldly fair;
Blush—if ever—faint and rare,
Flits like summer lightning there.

Little doth her face disclose—
Beautiful, but in repose—
Of the wealth her nature knows.

Lava fires undying glow
In unfathomed depths below,
Curtained by a wall of snow.

Gentle is she as a dove,
But by nature formed to move
Queen o'er all the realms of love,

A crown of constancy she wears,
As Blanc's cold heights, a thousand years,
Have pointed to the starry spheres.

A SERENADE.

Asleep, art thou, dearest, and dreaming of me?
Or hear'st thou my song as it floats up to thee?
Let thy hand gently loosen thy lattice, and
prove
That thy heart is awake to the call of thy love.

Not of gold, nor broad lands, to my darling I
sing,
But devotion the warmest and truest I bring;
No language so glowing, no music so rare,
A love can depict, that with mine can compare.

How radiant and pure shine the stars in the
sky,
While the great sleeping earth in deep shadow
doth lie;
But purer and deeper than either, must be
The passion that dwells in this bosom for thee.

Come, dearest, enrobed in thy mantle of snow,
A glimpse of thy form on thy lover bestow;
One wave of thy hand, and no longer alone,
His soul shall go forth to unite with thine own.

GERALDINE.

A SIESTA.

It happened—shall I e'er forget?
  One day that my young bride—
My own, my charming Geraldine,
  Sat sewing by my side.

The afternoon so lovely was,
  A walk with her I planned;
So having laid her needle by,
  We went forth hand in hand.

And wand'ring through the grand old woods,
  No words my joy could tell,
I thought within my soul, I ne'er
  Had loved her half so well.

At length we reached a dark retreat,
 Within the wood that slept,
Where often in our courting days,
 The trysting we had kept.

A fascinating, fearfully
 Romantic spot was this,
Upon the very edges of
 A dizzy precipice.

And old fantastic oaks, their arms
 Far o'er the brink did throw,
While a thread of limpid water leaped
 Into the gulf below.

And thus we stood—I gazing with
 Delight upon my dove,
For beauty is so precious in
 The being that we love.

When suddenly a step she took,
 I scarce had time to think;
She stooped to pluck a flower that grew
 Upon the fatal brink.

Transfixed I stood—I could not speak,
  Nor warning could bestow,
Alas! I saw her balance lost,
  She headlong fell below.

I shricked—I sprang to save her,
  When wide awake, I saw,
My nose, the laughing Geraldine,
  Was tickling with a straw.

DARKNESS.

Who hath not fellowed with despair—
Lost faith, and staggered—blind with doubt?
Nor felt that there were times when life's
Last joy seemed trampled out?

From such a wreck of ruined hopes,
Borne passive down a sweeping tide,
I turned, and through the darkness climbed
Far up a mountain side.

With heart all crushed as were its rocks,
And cold as seemed its silent frown,
I stood above that mountain rift,
And saw the moon go down.

I saw the moon go down, all pale
As her own kiss upon a shroud,
And then I heard the hollow wind,
Reverberating loud.

And I was all alone—alone.
  Upon that mountain wild and bare;
Ah! there are times when human hearts
  Will fellow with despair.

SUMMER LEAVES.

Summer leaves are dying,
Autumn winds are sighing,
Heralds sad of winter drear,
Howling round the stricken year.
Thus, soon our own short life has flown,
Youth's summer dream is o'er;
And the heart grieves o'er withered leaves,
Of joys that are no more—
Of joys that are no more.

TO A TRAVELER.

To wander o'er earth's strange lands,
  Obedient to a fate,
That points to some far distant prize,
  Thy toil to compensate;
To know that they are far away,
  Who are most dear to thee,
To miss their gentle, loving tones
  Spoken so tenderly;
To feel an utter loneliness,
  Though mingling with a throng,
With nothing left but memory,
  To feed thy heart upon;
In thy lone journey, wearied one!
  How sad thy soul must be,
With years that like an ocean lie,
  Between thy home and thee.

SAN PABLO.

OH! it is a night of beauty, that hath drawn
me thus away
From the glare of lighted chambers, with their
gallant guests and gay;
With a tenderness she greets me, for the wind
is sweet and low,
And like thoughts that move a quiet heart, its
pulses come and go.

See! the moon upon her cloud-car rides, of
pure and pearly gray,
Scatt'ring fragments of a shattered world of
silver o'er the bay,
And beyond the hills that fade away as distance
swims between,
There the tall sierra through the misty deep is
dimly seen.

Like a line of lurid lava glows the night-fire
on the strand,
While in creamy folds the white smoke lifts
itself above the land,
Till upon the breeze it rises to a region still
and clear,
Hanging like a wide and motionless pavilion in
the air.

Oh! it is a night of beauty, for the stars shine
sweetly down,
With a quiet gaze, as loving eyes have looked
into our own;
'Tis a night to charm the spirit with the touch
of other years,
Where embalmed lie youth's precious joys or
youth's most precious tears.

With a gentle hand adown the silent past she
guideth me,
As I move among the forms of things that long
have ceased to be;

And with sure, unerring footstep leadeth to a
scene of bliss,
Folded in the quiet shadows of a night the
twin to this.

I am standing by the wicket of a cottage, while
the moon
Throws her waste of liquid silver over all the
leafy June;
And with happy smile a maiden's young and
joyous face is seen,
Peeping through the shaded loopholes of the
ivy's glittering green.

From that home where sped her happy youth
in blest security,
With the perfect trust of innocence she cometh
forth to me;
Then with half directed footsteps we go wan-
d'ring through the shade
Of an aisle of pointed arches by the lofty cedars
made.

And I'm telling her a tale of love in earnest
words, and low
As the laugh of dimpled waters on their journey as they go;
And she listens without chiding me, nor bids
me to depart,
But comes trembling like a frighted bird, and
nestles near my heart.

But alas! I dream; the picture fast and faster
fades away,
And I wake amid the solitude that wraps the
lonely bay;
And my heart will not be comforted, but keeps
its store of love
For the golden land that lieth there—those
starry heights above.

LINES AT SEA.

ADDRESSED TO MY DAUGHTER.

On the bosom I'm borne of a calm summer
sea,
That seems to be sleeping as tranquilly,
As though the dark hurricane's wild rushing
sweep,
Had ne'er wakened to fury its waters so deep.

O'er these sweet peaceful waters we noiselessly
glide,
Save when a low breeze gently ripples the tide,
From the silvery crests of whose wavelets emerge
The low lulling sounds of the whispering surge.

To the far verge of ocean now wanders the eye,
To catch a faint image that looms in the sky,
'Tis a glimpse of the land, through the distance
that smiles,
Of the Florida coast with its thousand green
isles.

Now fades the broad daylight as evening draws
nigh,
And a single star peeps from its home in the
sky,
From its azure depths seeming a smile to bestow
On the grottos far down in the ocean below.

And I'm thinking, dear daughter, of thee, all
the while,
And the clear silvery radiance that beams in
thy smile;
May thy spirit through life be unclouded and
free,
And in peaceful repose, like this calm summer
sea.

AGNES.

Why, poor heart, so prone to cover,
  From each curious, searching eye,
Faintest trace that might discover
  What doth deepest in thee lie?
Dost thou nurse a secret sorrow—
  Hast thou found a joy serene?
Still thou seek'st from art to borrow
  Means to hide the fire within.

When upon thee joy is stealing,
  Bringing blissful ecstacy,
Close enshrined, the cherished feeling,
  Cunning heart, lies locked in thee.
Like the miser's hidden treasure,
  He so fondly gloats upon,
Deeper, sweeter is the pleasure,
  Thus to feel 'tis all thine own.

When, poor bleeding heart, expiring
  With the waste of hidden grief,
Efforts gentle, yet untiring,
  Fail to render thee relief,
Wilt thou not, thyself revealing,
  Faith at last in friends repose?
Vain persuasion! in concealing,
  Balm descendeth on thy woes.

MISERERE.

Down by the sea an old man sat,
 While on the rocks the rough sea broke.
"Tell me, I pray, what makes you look
 So sad," 'twas thus to him I spoke;
When, lifting up his silvery head,
And looking in my face, he said:

"Three years ago! alas! since then
 How many cherished hopes have fled;
And griefs that passed like storm-clouds by,
 And rosy joys that now are dead—
Those joys and griefs—a spectral throng,
That to the shadowy past belong.

"Three years ago! it seems a dream,
 But one whose forms are vivid yet:
That day is graven on my heart,
 A day I never shall forget;

For two were sitting by my side,
And one of them a plighted bride.

"A hand of each I held in mine,
The union of their hearts to bless,
And never shall I see again,
So mute but full a happiness.
He noble was, she very fair,
And one—aye both, my children were.

"But trials come, or soon or late,
To all who walk this realm of sin,
He had to struggle like the rest,
His fortune from the world to win.
For this he braved the stormy main–
We never heard of him again.

"For days—for months—a weary time,
Along the sea-side would she roam,
And with a deep, confiding faith,
She prayed and watched for him to come.
But by degrees she came to know
The dreadful measure of her woe.

"To the sea-side she went no more,
But meekly strove to meet her fate,
And with the same sweet grace performed
The simple duties of her state;
Through all that weary age of pain,
I never knew her to complain.

"Three days ago, a fresh-raised mound
Of earth, I saw with weeping eyes.
I try the mournful truth to hide,
But in my heart this record lies:
O'er him now rolls the sullen wave,
She fills a maiden's early grave."

NANNIE DARLING.

Nannie darling! Nannie darling!
  Ever blessed be this day,
That hath brought us to the altar,
  And thus given thee away.

That hath placed thee in my keeping;
  While my life blood courses warm,
Thee to comfort, thee to cherish,
  And to shield from every harm.

Ah! that eve I well remember,
  In the full leafed summer time,
When the dew was on the flowers
  Blooming round us in their prime.

Then 'twas in the tender moonlight,
  With my hand close grasping thine,
In my face you looked so fondly,
  As you promised to be mine.

And those days were bright and happy,
When the autumn time drew near,
When the yellow leaves were falling,
When the corn was in the ear.

When we roamed beside the river,
Heeding not how it might run,
Thinking only of the precious
Time, when we two would be one.

'Twas the same in piercing winter,
Or when oped the budding spring—
In the joy our hearts were nestling
That this blessed day would bring.

Yes, my darling, darling Nannie!
Ever blessed be this day,
That hath brought us to the altar,
And thus given thee away.

In the summer—in the autumn—
In the winter—in the spring,
I have loved my darling Nannie,
Best of every earthly thing.

Through the long years will I love her—
 Till the end of life shall be—
Till the moss is on my grave-stone—
 Aye! for all eternity!

OH! WOULD I WERE WITH THEE FOREVER!

OH! would I were with thee forever,
  Oh! would that we never might part,
That the joy that now thrills me might ever
  Fill up every vein of my heart.
I have traveled the fairy world over,
  I have tasted of many a bliss,
But 'twas madness to hope to discover
  The wealth of a moment like this.

Fate might point to the hour with her finger,
  That should tear me asunder from thee,
Yet my spirit would near thee still linger,
  And laugh at the harmless decree.
But no fancies like these will I cherish,
  Nor fear the sweet dream will not last--
That the bliss of this moment will perish,
  Or live but a dream of the past.

No! enough that I know thou art near me,
  Enough that I feel thou art mine—
As you gaze in my face, that you hear me,
  In accents responding to thine.
Then away with the future before me,
  Like a syren still singing of bliss,
Not the breadth of all time can allure me,
  While I live in a moment like this.

THE TWO VIOLETS.

A DREAM.

As by a murmuring stream I lay,
  Upon a shrubby knoll,
Soothed by the balmy breath of May,
  Sweet languor o'er me stole.

The bees' low hum, the leafy shade
  In stillness seemed to steep,
While drowsy zephyrs o'er me played,
  And whispered me to sleep.

And as with fancies oddly knit,
  My wandering senses teemed,
I lost me in their mazy flight,
  And thus it was I dreamed:

Methought two violets, side by side,
  Bloomed in a valley low;
In golden purple one was dyed,
  And one was white as snow.

The dews that on them lightly lie,
  The beams of heaven disperse,
While thus in friendly colloquy,
  The gentle pair converse:

"Fair sister," quoth the purple flower,
  "I'll tell thee why I fled
The gorgeous domes of pride and power,
    And sought this quiet shade.

"In ancient days, Rome foremost stood
  In science, arts, and laws,
Pleading, in her patrician blood,
  The mind's triumphant cause.

"'Twas here, where Tiber's waters flow
  Through banks with olives crowned,
And groves of citron trees, that throw
  Their odorous sweets around,

"I first upon the earth appeared,
An emblem fair, designed
To show that here the gods had reared
The garden of the mind.

"For no plebeian might appear
In garb of purple hue,
While from the royal robe I wear,
Its tint the toga drew.

"Here Learning's midnight lamp was fed
In broad-browed Wisdom's cell,
While Folly, oft rebuked, had fled,
In wilder climes to dwell.

"And Greatness then had reached the goal
That mortals might attain—
A lofty nobleness of soul,
More fitting gods than men.

"But when corrupt the state had grown,
And Luxury forged a chain
To drag the shaft of Virtue down,
That propped her golden reign,

"Rome yielded to the odious thrall
  That Sloth about her threw,
And Jove, offended at her fall,
  His tutelage withdrew.

"The badge of Greatness ceased to grace
  The broad and lofty brow,
And Honor lifted to her place
  The grov'ling and the low.

"And from that hour, the great of mind
  Retired from city strife,
Happy in rural peace to find
  The cordial balm of life.

"And I, the mind's pure emblem flower,
  Alike from crowds withdrew,
To bud and bloom from that same hour,
  In sweet seclusion too.

"Pray tell me, fairer sister, now,
  Why in this dreary shade,
In plain attire delightest thou
  To hide thy gentle head?"

Pausing, the other thus replied:
  "Sister, our fates are one;
To bloom unnoticed side by side,
  Where crime and tumult shun.

"Emblem of white-robed purity,
  My spotless petals tell
That where the wild wind wanders free,
  Fair Virtue loves to dwell.

"That where fresh fields and woods wave green,
  And purling streamlets roll,
The winning charms alone are seen,
  That catch the ingenuous soul.

"A truth we thus to man impart,
  That oft'nest will he find,
The noble mind, the virtuous heart,
  In rural life combined."

Just then, a storm o'ercast the day,
  And rolled the thunder deep,
And as the vision swam away,
  I started from my sleep.

But ere I shelter sought to find,
  Beneath yon hawthorn's shade,
I reasoned thus within my mind,
  And these reflections made.

With various views while all mankind
  On happiness are bent,
Striving with restless heat to find
  A haven of content,

My standard I have fixed so low,
  And yet withal so high,
Methinks that Heaven may still bestow
  The blessing ere I die.

Give me a mind with wisdom blest,
  A goodly stock of health,
A warm, true heart within my breast,
  And competence, not wealth.

With these, and those sweet, simple joys
  That rural charms supply,
In some sweet nook removed from noise,
  I'd wish to live and die.

OH, WOULD I WERE FREE!

"Oh, would I were free!" with what fervent
expression,
This thought gushes up from the wells of the
heart,
Or holds of its chambers a silent possession,
Ne'er in life's weary lease from its tenure to
part.

Methinks in the eye of that winged prisoner
yonder,
A look of sweet pitiful pleading I see,
And the song he is singing so plaintive and
tender,
Tells his captive heart's longing "Oh, would
I were free!"

"Oh, would I were free!" sighs with earnest
emotion,
The school-boy as out from his prison he
peers
O'er the fields and the woods from the breeze
all in motion,
And in the wild vesture that liberty wears.

When far from his mistress, thus speaks, too,
the lover,
While the star of the evening sheds on him
its ray,
"Oh! would that the days of my exile were
over,
That with joy I might break from my fetters
away."

And the wand'rer that has from his loved ones
been parted,
Between them long years and the great heav-
ing sea,
Awakes at the dead of the night broken-hearted,
And weeps on his pillow, "Oh, would I were
free!"

Alas! every creature from Adam descended,
Of lowly estate or exalted degree,
As the price to the boon of existence appended,
Feels the clasp of some fetter from which he'd be free.

Then patience, good brother! Time's waters are healing,
And every affliction that grieves us can cure,
But 'tis just when he pleases, his gifts he'll be dealing,
So let us be valiant and learn to endure.

Unwise 'tis to wish Time's swift pinions to hasten,
For sooner, perhaps, than we'd will it to be,
Death, that punctual old turnkey, will come to unfasten
The doors of our prison, and set us all free.

LIFE.

"FINIS CORONAT OPUS."

As tranquil joy to hearts long hopeless, so
  A golden sunset ends a day of storms;
And gay the craft on polar seas sore tost,
  Whose sails at last a rosy summer warms.
O happy life! in roughest pathways tried,
Whose steps at eve through peaceful valleys
    glide.

"Promise," above the cradle where he slept,
  Was writ in characters of glowing light;
Then happy, laughing childhood came, and then
  A youth of beauty crowned with all delight;
And twenty blooming summers, joining hands,
Led him at last to manhood's shining lands.

On dewy mound as stands a stag at morn,
  Snuffs the fresh mountain air and glances o'er
His boundless range of hazel, so with eye
  Dilated, and all eager to explore
The future's glimmering vista, once he stood,
While hope and faith stirred in his ardent blood.

Then forth into the world's wide lists he stepped,
  With life's grim foes to battle face to face,
Or, doffing casque and lance, with agile feet
  To struggle with the swiftest in the race;
Till, as on easy pinions of the wind,
He led the field and left all far behind.

Fortune with ready hand her treasures heaped,
  And strewed them broadcast in his path, and
    fame,
Loud pæans singing, crowned his brow with bays,
  And on a flood of honor bore his name;
Till incense, flung from censers swinging wide,
Seemed without perfume to his sated pride.

Then for a time he grasped the flying mane
  Of pleasure, vaulted on the frantic steed,

And skimmed the edges of her dizzy track;
Till love—the crowned queen—stayed his wild speed,
And turned his courser with a gentle hand,
To the sweet pastures of her flowery land.

In sunny lustre lies the home of love,
Connubial love, to holy flame akin,
Where joy forever on the threshold smiles,
And peace and sweet contentment dwell within,
And warm delights, but pure as summer rain;
Where passions rude for entrance knock in vain.

Here, with his other self, and offspring fair,
All gathered round him in that rare retreat,
He had his dream—forgetful of the years
That came and glided by with noiseless feet
O mortal joy! thy roots all shallow lie;
When blooming fairest, doomed alway to die.

As a low wind first ripples o'er a lake,
Then, piping on the mountain's piny comb,

Sweeps down the rocky gorge, a roaring blast,
  And lashes the chafed waters to a foam;
So bursts at once in dark and stormy strife,
Its first wild grief upon a joyful life.

A babe was born, but with its first faint cry,
  O God! the mother passed from earth away;
Then sudden night came down upon his soul,
  An icy darkness shutting out all day;
As if the living sun, struck dead in space,
Had left but one pale star to fill its place.

All listless lay the sullen sands of life
  As grain by grain they fell. A single day
Had touched with death the very face of time;
  While seasons all unheeded lapsed away;
A pulseless pause hung round the rolling years,
And brooded o'er a grief too deep for tears.

So, soon or late, to ashes crumble all
  The shrines where men their dearest treasures
    trust;
We build on frailty and the fabric falls;
  We grasp the apple but to find it dust.

And does this poor, unprofitable strife
To nothing lead? Is this the end of life?

Not so; it spins a thread beyond the grave,
  That links it fast to the eternal years;
Yet seems a short, imperfect fragment here,
  Till through the mists of death it reappears,
And shows, at last, the great Creator's plan
Of endless glory for his creature man.

And he, of whom these lines make record brief,
  Long prostrate lay, nor strove again to rise:
First on his spirit broke a feeble light,
  Then fell the holy glow of evening skies;
And resignation, bringing peace and rest,
Folded her wings and nestled in his breast.

As helmsman bold the breakers who hath braved,
  Looketh not back upon the dangers past,
Nor farther in where sleeps the sunny shore,
  But seaward points his steady prow at last;
So gained the good old man the open sea,
Whose waters mingled with eternity.

THE DOG AND THE CROCODILE.

SPANISH FABLE.

A kind, considerate crocodile,
Lay sunning in his favorite Nile;
As by the margin of the river—
To quench his thirst, or cool his liver—
A cur discreet, like master man,
Lapped the sweet water as he ran.
The cayman—oily chap—cried out,
"My friend, what canst thou be about?
Such haste shows plainly some delusion,
Most hurtful to thy constitution."
Dash still kept on, but spoke thus wise:
"Thanks for your very kind advice;
But I've a silly sort of notion,
I'd rather die of too much motion,
Than suffer you to solve the question,
If I be fit for your digestion."

AN EVENING SKETCH.

OH! what a marvellous perfection, hath
This summer eve put on! with subtle glide
It penetrates the soul, infusing there
A sense supreme of nature's peerless power.
The cumbrous harness of life's dusty way,
Falls at its touch; cares in oblivion sink,
And the freed spirit seems on rushing wings,
Rising through regions of the beautiful,
To catch some glimpses of its promised home.
  Low in the western sky, the sun hath sunk
Behind a gorgeous pyramid of clouds,
In purple robed, and edged with liquid gold;
And while upon the sweet and quiet earth,
That lies below, a softened shadow falls,
Some glittering lights still touch the lofty spire,
That mounts above the old cathedral's dome.
Time-honored pile! grey with the mould of years,
In venerable grandeur rooted there,

Like some bold beacon formed by nature's hand
In earth's young days, when the old hills were
born.
Hark! as from vasty lungs, a voice speaks
out,
In full, deep measured tones of earnestness.
For on the air—that seems to gather in
From far and near, the myriad sounds of earth,
And mingle them in one low, droning hum—
Solemn and deep the vesper bell sends forth
Its summons to the children of the vale.
And soon, obedient to the holy call,
They throng the way, now singly, now in groups.
Here mothers, smiling with maternal eyes,
Lead by the hand their sinless little ones;
And youths and maidens full of careless life,
And men in prime of days, with marks of care
Upon their brows, by turns come into view.
Others with tottering step, that tells of age,
With the poor cripple and the beggar join,
And all press forward, on one purpose bent—
To gain the gateway of the house of God.
Nor faded yet the golden summer eve!
A sweeter depth of beauty e'en she wears.

But nature hath no hold upon me more.
I ponder on that wondrous mystery
Of beauty—prayer—that brightening track of
light,
Up which the fervent soul may run—may fly,
And mount upon the wings of love, to hold
Communion with the denizens of heaven.

Lift up thy soul in grateful praise, O man!
That in thy hearts' deep sanctuary, lies
The source supernal of a beauty, far
Transcending all that nature can bestow;
For nature's but a ray of God's magnificence,
But God, himself, comes to the soul in prayer.

ROSALINDA.

Rosalinda! I love thee and thou lovest me,
The spell it is broken—our hearts are now free;
Free as streams that through rock-shrouded
darkness have run,
To burst into sunlight and mingle in one.

Long the heart-hidden mystery lay unrevealed,
And each from the other the secret concealed;
For we kept it enshrined—without word, with-
out look—
Between two silent natures, as in a sealed book.

With a root in each heart, yet together they
drew,
To become but one passion that secretly grew;
And in sunshine and darkness, with hopes and
with fears,
We have cherished the plant with the patience
of years.

Till at length in mute language it spoke from
the eyes;
We have told it in words, we have breathed
it in sighs;
We have rent the dull curtain that kept us apart,
And our vows have been ratified, heart against
heart.

Rosalinda! I love thee and thou lovest me,
But the wealth of our passion the world cannot
see,
For of all that's most prized what is hidden is
best,
If unveiled 'twould eclipse—'twould o'ershadow
the rest.

Who hath fathomed the earth and its treasures
all told?
Or hath counted the gems its dark caverns
enfold?
Who hath weighed all the gold in the glitter-
ing rills,
Or that's swelling the veins of the rock-hearted
hills?

Who hath dreamed not of beauties, for vision
too bright,
That lie hid in yon fathomless ocean of light?
Or knows not that yon little star distant and
dim,
Is a beautiful world lost forever to him?

Rosalinda! I love thee and thou lovest me,
We are floating in light other eyes cannot see,
'Tis all darkness to them, yet to us it appears
To illumine every path in this valley of tears.

NOW WHEN THE SHADES OF SUMMER EVE.

Now when the shades of summer eve begin to
close,
And night to weary mortals soon shall bring
repose,
The gentle stars shall shine on me,
And light the path that leads to thee,
And light the path—light the path that leads
to thee.

Upon my ear, as through the dewy woods I
hie,
The whip-poor-will's low liquid note falls plain-
tively,
Till love's low greeting welcomes me,
Where ends the path that leads to thee,
Where ends the path—ends the path that leads
to thee.

LOST AT SEA.

Far out upon the dreary waste
  Of ocean waters, dark and deep,
Where boundless space embosomed lies,
  By silence nursed to sleep:

Lifted above those awful depths,
  That dream in endless night below,
Where stillness ever reigns—where waves
  Break not, nor tempests blow;

A solitary object swings
  Upon the stately swelling sea—
A human creature, wrestling with
  A frightful destiny.

A shattered spar he clings to, but
  With feeble hold, that drowning man;
The strong stout heart no longer nerves
  His form, grown weak and wan.

Thrice hath he seen the sun come up,
And thrice sink down into the sea,
As struggling, life's frail hold to keep,
He nears eternity.

Fear's icy zone his soul hath passed,
Its terrors now bring no dismay;
E'en hope, that for a season cheered
His heart, hath passed away.

Great God! can thought e'er comprehend
The height and depth of such a woe,
When the spent flesh almost hath ceased
Of suffering to know?

Feebly he lifts his dying eyes,
As, from the cold and quiet sea,
The moon, upon night's pearly shell,
Rises in majesty.

Why throbs again life's ebbing tide?
Why gleams that wild light in his eye?
On the horizon's glittering line,
A sail looms in the sky.

Nearer she comes—and nearer still,
  Her masts—her very shrouds are seen;
In mercy will she yet ride o'er
  The space that lies between?

To wave a signal with his hand,
  He gathers all his feeble force;
Alas! his only hope expires;
  She keeps upon her course.

No watchful eye that signal sees,
  No friendly hand is stretched to save,
Too much! frail nature can no more,
  He sinks into the wave.

And wailing winds his dirge shall sing,
  Nor sadder could the requiem be,
O'er him who rests in dreamless sleep,
  Beneath the cold blue sea.

DEATH.

I.

Cruel Death! relentless foe!
Striking down with crushing blow,
What our hearts cling closest to;
The sharp—the agonizing pang,
Thy shaft doth give,
To those that live,
Is keener, deeper, bitterer than
The anguish of the dying man.
Past are his pains,
When through his veins,
With subtle speed is driven,
Quick as th' electric flash of heaven,
The freezing poison of thy fang.
He, thy malice now defies,
He who still and pallid lies,

Like a marble effigy, upon his funeral bier;
Turn, turn away,
From the cold clay,
In bleeding hearts your triumph lies, not here.
No more upon that placid brow,
With all thy torturing arts, wilt thou
Excite a frown.
With his last moan,
The mortal throe was o'er,
Now he can feel
Thy deadly steel
No more.
See, all the while,
A happy smile
Plays round his lips and seems to tell,
His spirit light,
Has winged its flight
To heaven, with its God to dwell.

II.

Death! here's your prey—this mourning troop
Of friends, this weeping band
Of kindred, too, who stand
Around the grave, a wretched group.

While on the hushed and silent air
Breathe the low wailings of despair,
Wrung from yon pale and wasted one,
Whose tottering step and faded cheek,
And sunken eye, too plainly speak
The havoc thou hast done.
Complete thy work, O Death!
Snatch away her feeble breath.
Let thy spell about her creep,
Shroud her in thy icy sleep.
She's thy captive now—art sure?
Is she thine for evermore?
Blind, indeed, O Death! thou art,
To the bright immortal part;
All that's left thee for thy portion of the prize,
Is the cold insensate clay,
While her spirit's gone away,
To the dwellings of the angels in the skies.

UNSELFISH LOVE.

In woody dell, where dark boughs meet
O'er waters murmuring at my feet,
'Mid depths of mystic shade I lie,
And muse on life's sad mystery.
Alas! why should my lips disclose
The secret of my bosom's woes?
Why even by a look reveal
The passion that for her I feel?
Some chord within her heart may lie,
Already tuned to sympathy,
That only needs the master tone,
To wake the music of its own.
But had not best that answering lay,
Another touch than mine obey?
One in whose love she'd haply be
More blest than sharing life with me.
Alas! I know no other dwells
On earth, up from whose bosom wells

For her, so warm, but pure a flood
Of deep, intense solicitude;
And all of wealth heaven could bestow,
All that of fame man's heart might know,
All he might glean from earth, in fine,
I'd barter all to call her mine.
But would I not, for wealth or fame
That fancy's wildest dream could name,
Beguiled by self, consent to throw
One shadow on her cloudless brow.
No! rather let my secret rest
Forever buried in my breast,
Unless sweet proofs my senses move,
That she'd delight in my poor love.

DOWN BY SILENT WATERS.

Down by silent waters,
  Stretching far away
In the misty distance,
  Sat we one sweet day,

Near the grassy margin
  Of those waters still,
In the shadow of the
  Overhanging hill.

One sweet day in Autumn,
  Sat we there alone,
Hushed the heart of nature,
  Hushed as were our own.

Silence all around us,
  Silence in the air,
Silence o'er the waters—
  Silence everywhere.

Till the full enchantment
  On our spirits fell,
With a depth of meaning,
  Words can never tell;

Till with mute emotion,
  Hand in hand was laid—
Vows the purest, truest,
  Silently were made;

Vows, outliving seasons
  Fraught with joys or tears,
Standing like pale tombstones
  Over buried years—

Of a life the record—
  All too bright to last—
Pointing to a shadow
  In the spectral past;

Years that back have brought me,
  As on that sweet day,
To these silent waters
  Stretching far away,

From their grassy margin,
  There reposing still,
In the shadow of the
  Overhanging hill.

Silence all around me,
  Silence in the air,
Silence o'er the waters—
  Silence everywhere.

Shroud-like while it wraps me,
  Ling'ring here alone,
Seems the heart of nature
  Dead as is my own.

FORTUNE'S FAVORITE.

"THE HEART KNOWETH ITS OWN BITTERNESS."

How poorly doth the shallow world
  Our hearts' dark currents scan!
Methinks I hear the thoughtless crowd
  Exclaim, "Oh, happy man!

"Life's richest prizes thou hast won,
  Friends, fortune, and a name,
For to the very dregs thou'st drained
  The honied cup of fame."

Ah! could they penetrate this breast,
  And mark the gloom that's there,
Earth's humblest son would not exchange
  His lot for one so drear.

Ah! Mary, thou hast left me here,
With naught thy place to fill,
For the sunshine of my life went out
When thy warm pulse stood still.

Men look with envy at my life,
The honors that are mine,
Heaven knows I'd freely give them all
For one sweet smile of thine.

Now through the world's admiring throngs
Indifferent I move;
What is man's feeble praise to me?
I've nothing left to love.

The laurel wreath upon my brow
An idle mockery seems;
Thy tenderness was more to me
Than glory's wildest dreams.

I cannot call thee back to life;
Thou'rt gone for evermore;
Yet do I feel that we shall meet
When life's dull season's o'er.

And in eternal bonds re-joined,
  When the last trump shall sound,
Roaming through sunny paths of peace,
  Our spirits will be found.

LONGINGS.

'Tis a flower divinely rare,
I've been seeking everywhere,
'Neath the ocean depths of air.

Where the broad earth sweeps away
In the glimmering dawn of day,
Searching still my footsteps stray..

Round me streams the amber sun,
Oft as in my haste I run,
But my task is never done.

Sometimes when with glittering light,
Stars shine o'er me cold and bright,
Search I hopeless through the night.

And the morning young and fair,
Dawns again to find me there,
With a spirit crushed with care.

Climb I then the cliffs that rise,
Lost in folds that veil the skies,
Hoping there to seize my prize.

Where the waters ebb and flow
O'er their pebbly depths below,
I have dreamed the flower might grow;

And with power that fancy gave,
Fathomed every ocean cave,
But it bloomed not 'neath the wave.

Sea and land, sunshine and shade,
Mountain proud and lowly glade,
Fruitless search through all I've made.

Oft I've scanned the brazen sky,
Pond'ring on the mystery,
Till my eyes were strained and dry.

Then to earth I've turned again—
Fruitful soil, where grief and pain
Thrive in tears as plants in rain.

Life is nearly spent and gone,
Weary grows my heart, and lone,
Shall I call the flower my own?

Ne'er on earth that joy may be,
Only will it bloom for me,
On thy shores, eternity!

A WINTER ELEGY.

IMITATION OF GRAY.

THE wintry blast howls through the forest grey,
The leafless branches rattle on each tree,
The withered leaves in eddies whirl away,
And stricken nature meditates with me.

Now lulls in lessening gusts the wind away,
And sounds in stagnant silence seem tc freeze,
Save where yon wild stream dashes on its way,
Or whisp'ring sedges catch the dying breeze.

Save that from yonder venerable tree,
The raven croaks her melancholy strain,
To such as heedless sail o'er life's smooth sea,
Nor dream that death is slumbering on the main.

Beneath these aged oaks—these hoary boughs,
  Where daily now the white man toils for
    food,
The smoky wigwam knew its simple joys,
  Or round its fires the Indian warriors stood.

The thunder-smiting crash, nor falling pine,
  Nor roaring whirlwind, nor the battle yell,
Nor arrow's whiz, nor strong bow's twanging
    line,
  Shall ever break their slumber's heavy spell.

For them no more the martial fire shall burn,
  When some old chieftain tells his battles
    o'er,
Nor dusky bride await her lord's return,
  Or fearful, dread lest he return no more.

Oft through the thicket sped the fatal dart,
  The bounding deer oft felt the unerring
    stroke,
How wild and free throbbed each unfettered
    heart!
  How glad their shout the forest silence broke!

Let not refinement eriticise their ways,
Their vengeful hate—their thirst for bloody fame,
Nor cultured man withhold his meed of praise,
For vengeance, then, and virtue, were the same.

CONFIDENCE.

IMITATION OF SHENSTONE.

Ye damsels, blithe, happy, and free!
With hearts unacquainted with love;
Ye shepherds, who pipe o'er the lea!
Content with your lambkins to rove,
In you I can never confide,
Gay maidens and light-hearted swains,
For I very well know you'll deride
The sweet secret my bosom contains.

But I'll hie me away to yon wood,
In whose covert the low cooing dove,
Undisturbed in her sweet solitude,
Ever warbles her lament of love.
And I'll mingle my sighs with the strain,
In which her lost mate she bewails;
To the rocks and the trees I'll complain,
For such confidants never tell tales.

When I peep in the streams as I pass,
  Alas! what sad changes appear;
The lilies 'tis easy to trace,
  But the roses no longer are there.
Now can I be blamed that I'm sad,
  That my mirth and good humor are flown?
Should I not be ashamed to seem glad,
  When my Lubin—sweet shepherd—is gone?

When free with my Lubin to stray,
  And list the sweet truths he would own,
The hours so quick flew away,
  They were past ere I thought them begun;
Since his voice I no longer may hear,
  I am lost in abstraction profound;
I sit by the hour unaware
  Of a thing that is passing around.

They may tell me my Lubin's untrue,
  Nor cares his lost Delia to see,
That his heart he has promised to Sue,
  That was long ago given to me;
But such slanders I will not believe,
  Foul envy is all that they prove;

For my Lubin would never deceive
  The lassie that once fixed his love.

Then listen, thou soft-scented gale!
  Nor hasten unkindly away,
Till thou hear'st from my lips a true tale,
  To be borne to my Lubin this day:
Oh, tell him no other than he,
  Can lift from my bosom its pain!
Oh, tell him to come back to me,
  And I shall be happy again!

MARGARET.

I HAD a dream, a pleasant dream, last night,
And much I marvel that so vividly,
By memory's untrimmed light,
Should glow the image of an old delight,
And come with such a freshness back to me.

The village where my boyhood glided by,
I saw reposing, as in days of yore,
Beneath an evening sky;
And like a low and plaintive melody,
The quiet picture touched my soul once more.

Then joy stole o'er me, like a thought of love,
The outline of the pale new moon to see,
Poised in the vault above,
As floats a feather from a snow-white dove,
For thus she said, "Thy wish shall answered
be."

The wish, unuttered, only lived in thought,
And yet a pleasing change came o'er the scene,
Most marvellously wrought—
A fair-haired girl close to my side seemed brought,
And wandered with me o'er the village green.

From her sealed lips no soft confession fell,
No word of love I yet had dared to breathe her,
Why 'twas I could not tell,
But hushed our simple hearts seemed by a spell,
Though beating such a sweet tattoo together.

I never have forgotten Margaret,
She was the gentlest thing I ever knew,
So serious, and yet
Sweet mirth sometimes came like a sparkling jet,
From out her eyes of bright, but earnest blue.

Without a cloud her morn of life had been,
And to my own its sunny light imparted,

Our future all unseen—
So woven into one our hearts seemed then,
We never dreamed that we could e'er be parted.

Alas! that those first golden blooms of love—
Those promises of youth so true and tender—
Should perishable prove,
Or only live in dreams, the heart to move;
Scant tribute to those dear old times to render.

Swift years, ah, whither flown! I know not now
The country e'en where Margaret is dwelling;
Mayhap her form lies low
Beneath the turf where the wild daisies grow,
Some time-worn stone her simple story telling.

Peace to thee, Margaret; peace, where'er thou art,
In earthly home, or heaven, hence summoned early;
Yet ere from thee I part,
I'll breathe once more, peace to the gentle heart
Of her, whom, long ago, I loved so dearly.

My dream is o'er; nay, is't not one long dream,
This life of mine? phantasmagoria, all
    Its lights and darks must gleam,
Until eternity's bright morning beam
To deathless life my slumbering soul shall call.

THE BRIDAL MORN.

Upon a grassy slope that scarce had given
All its fresh moisture to the morning sun,
But still some sparkling drops contrived to
 screen
From the warm wooings of his amorous beams,
A youth, whose fair unfurrowed brow pro-
 claimed
A fresh young soul, free from all taint of care,
Among a joyous group conspicuous stood.
His clear bright eye, from which, at other times,
A glorious energy oft shone, with look
Of fond and earnest tenderness, now gazed
Upon another and a fairer form—
One that with fluttering heart, in dubious maze
Of mingled joy and fear, stood half unnerved,
Yet happy by his side. Yes, happy both!
And in the changing scenes of after years,

Whate'er betide, this of all others will
Remembered be. For 'twas the bridal day
Of this young pair—an Indian summer morn,
That veiled itself in haze of dreamy blue,
Sleeping so stilly, that the rustlings of
The dropping leaves, like whispers seemed into
The ear to glide. While all unconscious of
The scene, or viewing, in its mirroring face,
Reflexes only of their own light hearts,
This merry troop saw not the shadow cast
By melancholy there—that spectre dim,
That follows nature wheresoe'er she dwells,
Sadd'ning her every smile—but in a mood
Of jollity, chatting in under tone
Of whispered mirth, or half checked gayety,
Toward the chapel bent their lightsome steps.
And to the portal as they nearer drew,
That dimly brought to view the sacred aisle,
The little birds up in the old oak trees
Poured forth a welcome in a stream of song;
While breathing from the sanctuary, came
Issuing forth, the fragrance of fresh flowers,
That pious hands had on the altar placed.
And now from yon old lofty granite pile,

The merry, merry wedding bells are ringing,
And a gay and lively phantasy seem singing,
As if a spirit from the realms of joy and light,
Human hearts had come to ravish with delight,
Or rather seemed it only to impart
The faithful echo of the bridegroom's joyous
heart.
But a voice seems wailing from the depths of
time,
And it mingles, oh! how sadly, with that chime,
Scattered fragments of a wild prophetic rhyme.

Chime.

Happy, happy, happy youth!
Seeing with the eye of truth,
And proclaiming all things fair,
That the lovely earth doth wear,
With a spirit pure and free,
Loving life's reality,
Time no terrors hath for thee.

Voice.

There's joy in thy smile, and there's light in
thine eye,
Then why struggles up from thy bosom that
sigh?

Why trembles thy hand, and why blanches thy
cheek?
Happy heart! in those whispers does joy seem
to speak?

Chime.

As to-day thou know'st no sorrow,
So 'twill likewise be to-morrow,
So with each succeeding sun,
Till life's pleasant course be run.

Voice.

Now from the fair east, like a warrior bold,
The sun rideth forth in his armor of gold,
But ere to their rest the winged songsters shall
hie,
More shadows than one shall pass over the sky.

Chime.

Passing all things fair is she,
Whose heart, fond youth, is pledged to thee;
Aye! lovely as in snowy white,
The daisies on a mountain height.

Voice.

A violet to place in the hair of the bride,
Fresh plucked from the bed of green turf at
her side,

'Tis bright as the tints of the morning to-day,
To-morrow 'twill droop, soon to perish away.

Chime.

Life's a gently flowing stream,
Life's a sweet untroubled dream,
Life's a string of sunny hours,
Bright as dew-drops on the flowers,
Life is gold without alloy,
Full of hope, and love, and joy.

Voice.

Hear ye not the waters moan
In a low and wailing tone,
Ever murmuring on the air,
Joy is sister-twin to care?
Doth not every thing betray
Lights all crossed with shadows grey—
Brightest blossoms everywhere,
Saddened by the blights they bear?
And shall human hearts go free,
When naught that springs from earth can flee
The universal destiny?

Chime.

In the spring time when sweet May
Strewed the fields with flow'rets gay,

Up and down on airy wing,
Two gay birds went wandering;
And first a wreathy flight they weave,
As loath their wild retreat to leave,
But soon a bolder flight they take,
And skim along the quiet lake,
Or upward spring on high to soar,
Till back to earth they dip once more,
Again to poise—to dart—to glide,
Forever by each other's side.
Oh! in how wild a wantoning
They pass the merry days of spring!
Youth and maiden, plighted pair,
These two birds your shadows are,
In their May-day flight ye see
Your own unclouded destiny.

Voice.

Hark! the winds of winter sigh,
Listen! oh, how mournfully!
As o'er blighted fields they stray,
Murmuring, summer's passed away—
Summer with its sun and showers,
Grass and dew-drops, birds and flowers—
Offspring of the fleeting hours;

All are gone; and hovering there,
Like sickly phantoms in the air,
Shadows now all grey and cold,
As in a shroud the earth enfold.
And whence that low and plaintive cry—
That one sad note of agony?
On yonder stript and withered bough,
Alas! the lonely mourner now—
The minstrel whose wild notes of spring,
No more through woodland haunts shall ring,
To fly the spot attempts in vain
And to his perch returns again;
To linger there disconsolate
Where last he saw his dying mate.
Alas! full soon all hearts shall know
That joy must ebb as well as flow,
For never yet was nursed a bliss
That bore not fruits of bitterness.

* * * * * * *

The birds have ceased their caroling,
The bride has worn the wedding ring,
The nuptial blessing has been given,
And registered the rite in heaven.

Now stay thee, Time! why farther run,
When joy's bright goal this day is won?
Or if thy course must onward be,
Why drag these happy hearts with thee?

* * * * * * *

Alas! it was an idle prayer,
That day has flown so bright and fair;
And many more that sped as fast,
Gone down to slumber in the past.

TO MISS K. M.

ON HER WEDDING DAY.

A BRIGHTER morn, O maiden!
  Now on thy pathway beams,
Than ever shed its joy on thee,
  In fancy's wildest dreams.
The earth has grown more beautiful,
  A balmier air it breathes,
As round thy heart a chaplet bright
  Of sunny hopes she wreathes.

Oh, ever joyful destiny
  Of those who wed with love—
A shadow of the perfect state
  Of souls that dwell above!
Glad tidings, gentle maiden!
  This blissful morning brings,
From true affection's dropping dew,
  An endless verdure springs.

Then sweetly glide thy hours, and when
  Long years have passed away,
May every memory be bright,
  That's linked with this bright day.
Perchance, you too, may sometimes cast
  A thought of kindly hue,
On him who from his exile pens
  These simple lines to you.

CAST DOWN.

Cold, listless, dull! what o'er my soul hath
come,
That day by day, emotionless and dumb,
Chained to the earth, a helpless weight I lie?
Why, living still, a very stone am I?

I hear—I feel—the same broad earth I see,
Myself, a parcel of the mystery!
All still remains to point the soul to God,
And yet my heart is dead, and I a clod.

He only who gave nature life and law,
And out of nothing deigned my soul to draw,
With vital flame can bid this rush-light burn,
His hand withdrawn—to nothing I return.

He, then, the King, o'er seas that hath com-
mand,
Who holds them in the hollow of his hand,

Who lets the tempest loose, or by whose will
The angry waters and the waves are still;

He 'tis, whose rule the gathering ages own,
Who man's proud nature brings in mercy down,
That from his deep abasement he may see,
Abandoned thus, how poor a wretch is he.

Re-light in me, my God! thy fire divine.
Construct anew this prostrate wreck of thine!
One look of love shall all-sufficient be,
To lift it up from earth to heaven and Thee.

YELLOW FEVER.

The fever fiend! the fever fiend! he comes,
make haste to fly;
Fly all who can, nor stay to swell the low despairing cry
Of yon poor crouching multitude, whose time
has come to die.

With noiseless tread he stalks among his unresisting foe,
Invisible his murd'rous blade, but sure the fatal
blow,
As right and left, with steady hand, he strikes
his victims low.

What frightful thing is this that can the strong
man thus restrain,
Can make him like an infant, weak, can fill his
bones with pain,
His blood can clog with poison, and with madness fire his brain?

He cometh now—whence cometh he? no living
man can tell—
We know him only by the slain about our
hearths that fell,
By the rumbling of the dismal hearse, the toll-
ing of the bell.

All weathers are alike to him, he scorns the
tempest's rage,
With dauntless front he walks abroad, a deadlier
war to wage,
A dark day's work that night he writes upon
his bloody page.

Oh! one would think, so sweet a breeze as
this from off the sea,
With not a cloud to mar the azure continuity,
Might gain one day of grace at least—alas! no
grace grants he.

A score of sunny days are linked by nights,
oh! how serene,
With skies of strange transparency where not
a cloud is seen,

But fiercer grows the slaughter now than ever
it had been.

No day, no night, no time of storm, no calm,
no sun, no shower,
Can stay the fatal pestilence, nor battle with
its power,
Until the Lord of hosts relent, and mark its
final hour.

HOPE AND DESPAIR.

Hope.

Mortals, come along with me,
We will roam futurity.
All is happy, all is free,
In the bright futurity.
Sons of earth, rejoice, rejoice!
Hear ye not Hope's cheering voice?
Mortals mortals, will ye come?
Hope invites you to her home.
Hark! I touch the trembling string,
Rich celestial raptures sing,
The unborn hour alone can bring.
Ye shall loiter in my bowers,
Shall eat my fruits, shall pluck my flowers,
Shall drink the nectar of my rill,
While odors soft your senses fill.
No glossy berries tempting glare,
To fill your veins with poison there;

No hidden bee with sudden sting,
One momentary pang shall bring;
There no unwholesome nauseous drop,
With bitterness shall dash your cup,
For in my bright enchanted isle,
Grief shall grow glad and sorrow smile.
Look at the stars in yonder sky,
They shine not half so bright as I;
Yon ruined tower, yon aged tree,
The moon is veiling mellowly,
With molten silver landscape laves,
And glitters on the dancing waves.
But mortals, mortals, turn to me,
Far brighter is futurity.

Despair.

Out! out! wanton sprite, thou could'st never yet dare
To face the dark lowering scowl of Despair.
Thy promises vanish like mists from the air,
And man finds a haven at last in Despair.
Loud, solemn, and deep tolls yon old chapel bell,
It is ringing thy requiem—Hope, fare thee well!

Come along, come along with me, children of clay,
Your life's like a shadow that passeth away;
Yon sun as he rose seemed to smile on your birth,
But ye mingle at e'en with the dust of the earth.
O mortal, O mortal, come wander with me,
Along the wild shore of the dark rolling sea,
And hear from the depths of my grim rocky cave,
The dash of the breaker, the roar of the wave.
When clouds in black volumes roll over the sky,
And the storm in its fury sweeps fearfully by,
Unmoved thou shalt smile at the terrors of night,
And brood o'er thy woes with a savage delight.
When the thunder-clap bursts, and the red lightnings gleam,
Thou shalt mingle thy shrieks with the sea-bird's wild scream,
And thy laugh, like a demon's, shall ring through the air,
Oh! fierce is the triumph that waits on Despair.

Observe yonder planet—the queen of the even,
How proudly she walks through the dark vault
of heaven,
See! see! she is nearing the line of yon height,
And now she sinks down on the bosom of
night.
O man! in that star thy dark destinies gloar,
Like her a brief moment your spirit may soar,
Like her, too, a frowning horizon you'll near,
And seek for repose on the night of Despair.

Hope.

Gentle spirit, come away,
Come into the dawning day.
Darkness all around thee lies,
Deepening for the sacrifice.
Ruin waits to stab thee there,
On the altar of Despair.
One more victim still to gain
For the realms of endless pain.
Come, freed spirit, come away,
Come into the dawning day.
Erst to lure thee and to save,
Dreams of earthly bliss I gave,

Now to earth no longer cling,
Earth is but a hollow thing.
All the joy, and all the woe
It can give, like shadows go;
But thou shalt, when they're all gone,
Lean on me, poor lonely one;
Gently will I soothe thy pain,
And thy strength renew again,
Train thy wings to soar with me
To the land I promised thee;
Far away beyond the skies,
In an endless spring it lies.
Spirit, come then, come with me,
Rest thou in eternity.

AFTER AN ILLNESS.

How quiet my eye, and how pale my cheek,
My breathing how low, and my pulse how
weak,
I struggle to lift up my head, but in vain,
It feebly sinks back on its pillow again.

But the fire is quenched that but yesterday
Was drying the streams of my life away,
And like the cool wave as it kisses the shore,
The fresh tide of health is returning once more.

From the wild dreams of phrensy my spirit
awakes,
And on me the morn of sweet consciousness
breaks,
To the music of earth once again I'm alive,
And my heart overflows as my senses revive.

My friends are about me, how quiet their tread
As they softly steal up to the side of my bed,
To take my thin hand in their own to be
pressed,
And with words of encouragement gladden my
breast.

Come pillow me up in my easy chair,
And let me be placed where the pure fresh air
Of heaven, may play o'er my fevered skin,
And woo the red streams from their fountain
within.

Bright, beautiful world! once again I behold
Thy glorious day-sky of azure and gold,
Thy mountains, thy trees, thy gay streams, thy
green sod,
All preaching alike of the glory of God.

Why dost thou, my soul, at life's ills so repine,
And forget all the wonderful gifts that are
thine?
Be mindful that God in his wisdom employs
Afflictions as showers to freshen our joys.

MEMORY OF CHILDHOOD.

Come, Memory! mistress as thou art
Of sweetest chords to move my heart,
Who canst beguile each wayward mood,
That grieves my own loved solitude,
Come, let me nestle close to thee,
My sweet companion, Memory;
And lie entranced from hour to hour,
Within thy world-excluding bower.
Aladdin-like thy lamp supplies
What most my soul hath learned to prize,
Its piercing, penetrating ray
Illumes life's dim and faded way,
And through the shadowy haze of years,
The long-forgotten past appears—
The Past, far pleasanter to me
Than dark, unknown Futurity,
Where hope and fear alternate rise,
To rule her ever-changing skies.

Sweet mistress of the lonely hour,
By thee detained with dreamy lore
Of other days, I seem again
Transported to my native glen;
Again I frisk through forests wild,
Where once I roved a happy child,
Light, careless, gay, and ever free
As the inconstant honey bee,
That wand'ring on from flower to flower,
Lights on a hundred in an hour.
Thus does wild youth its sports pursue,
And ever flies to what is new;
Pleasures are only won to cloy,
Or dropped to seize some brighter joy.
With thee, sweet Memory, for my guide,
Thus back to fairy-land I glide,
Where I was wont from meadows gay,
To cull the brightest flowers of May,
Or over hill and valley hie,
To catch the bright-winged butterfly.
But if, while innocence and truth
Smiled on my bright and happy youth,
Some pigmy grief chanced to pursue—
For childhood has its sorrows too—

I'd sit me down and weep the while,
But soon would come a cheery smile,
That quickly chased my tears away,
And I once more was blithe and gay.

Thus gushes free my heart in praise,
When I review those dear old days,
When virtue with her mild control,
Guided aright my untaught soul,
Kept from my path all guilt or care,
That after many a stormy year,
I yet might find, at least in thee,
One blameless joy, dear Memory!

THE DYING GIRL TO HER LOVER.

A SONG.

Too late, ah! dearest one, too late,
  Thou comest to thine own again;
Alas! to die is my sad fate,
  Why, why must bliss thus end in pain?
They parted us—ah! doom too sure
  To leave me thus in grief to pine!
Thy fondness now can ne'er restore
  This pale and wasted form of mine.

But better thus, at life's last hour,
  To know that thou dost love me still,
Than linger on, a faded flower,
  Touched by a blight that could not kill.
Fast fade those features dear of thine,
  No more I mark thy anxious eye,
Then press thy warm sweet lips to mine,
  And let me thus in rapture die.

MORNING.

'TIS day, 'tis day, for hark! I hear
The joyous voice of chanticleer;
He tosses high his coral crest,
He flaps his wings, he ruffs his breast,
And proudly seems the while to say,
As loud he winds his clarion gay,
"I'm the glad herald of the day."
The first faint gleam of grey now flies
In silver streaks athwart the skies,
Night's sable veil asunder tears,
When lo! yon eastern height appears,
With web of light about it spread
And stars thick clustering round its head.
But these, like pearls on field of jet
That grace a queenly coronet,
At every instant grow less bright,
And one by one dissolve in light,
At whose soft touch night's paling woof
Shrinks from the heavens' o'erarching roof.

And o'er yon hills, whose bases lie
In formless, dim uncertainty,
But rising from the shadowy night,
Their outline lies in glimmering light,
Long wavy clouds are seen to flare
Like pennants streaming to the air.
Through every hue their color flies,
As when the changing dolphin dies;
A rosy blush an instant seen—
An orange glows where it had been,
And yellow melting into green.
And as we mark each flying hue,
That tender, mild, delicious blue,
That only when the skies are clear
May tinge the mellow atmosphere,
Appears, absorbing all the rest,
And smiling spreads from east to west.
A golden glory far and near,
Now fires the orient hemisphere,
A broader, brighter circle throws,
Until from pole to pole it glows,
And blazing Phœbus, upward whirled,
Sheds lustre o'er a waking world.
But turn from Phœbus and the skies,

New beauties in the landscape rise.
Upon the wood-sprung zephyr-tide,
The mists career the mountain side;
And setting o'er yon dark ravine,
Through their grey depths no longer seen,
In crowded phalanx there await
The certain issue of their fate;
For in a thousand shadowy forms,
They vanish as the morning warms.
And tumbling down the broken steep,
Bright sparkling cascades headlong leap,
Which coursing, as they fall below,
The winding vale, their murmuring flow
Commingles with the melody
Of warbling throats from brake and tree,
And far off sheep-bell's tinkling note,
And sound of woodman's axe remote,
And insects' droning symphony.
While the shrill mountain clarion clear,
That quivering cleaves the dewy air,
Startles fleet echo from the woods,
Her shades and dreamy solitudes,
Who, shy, retreats the vale along,
Yet with gay mischief on her tongue,

Repeats each sound with sweet decay,
Fainter, as fast she flies away.
Now let us climb to yonder height,
And give expansion to the sight.
O'er rolling woods, whose stately trees
In bending grace obey the breeze,
The ravished eye dilated bounds
O'er miles of cultivated grounds,
Fields of ripe grain and meads in flower,
With cottage homes all dotted o'er—
Homes that repay for all their toil,
The happy tillers of the soil.
Such scenes the generous soul must fire,
And elevating thoughts inspire.
Who can behold so fair a show,
Nor feel his breast with fervor glow?
With tenderer charities inclined
T'ward all the race of human kind;
And t'ward that bounteous God above,
Who ever guards us with his love,
A gratitude without alloy,
For all the blessings we enjoy.

NIGHT.

Night! gentle queen of life's far sweeter half,
Mild mistress of the meditative mind!
To thee, beneath whose deep enchanting power,
The minstrels of all ages and all climes
Have their enamored souls poured forth in song;
To thee, while music strikes her stirring chords,
That in sweet modulations rise and fall
Upon the evening medium still, I'll weave
A simple lay.
The sunset glow is passed,
The purple eve has faded into grey,
And twilight dim has gone to hide herself
Within thy folding robe of silence and
Repose. The stars that speak of heaven and God,
Are clustered in thy bosom: the new moon—
Pale crescent—sits upon thy brow, and o'er
The noiseless world a silvery lustre sheds,

Soft as the mellow calm that crept at eve
Through Eden's happy groves. And not a
sound
Is heard save such as swell the melody
That saturates, like balm of summer flowers,
The depths of nature—save the murmurings of
The distant waterfall, the droning hum
Of insects, or the whisperings of the breeze.
Oh! what a time to listen to the voice
Of Memory, as she whispers of the past,
Once loved so well, but now, alas! no more.
The troops of friends that thronged the busy
field,
Through which life's pathway wound, where
are they now?
Gone from the earth like mists from off the
hills.
Some lie unhonored in a stranger land,
With not a stone to mark their last sad place
Of rest; others have found a watery grave,
Food for the monsters of the deep; while some
Still bear the onerous charge of life, tired of
Their burdens, yet reluctant to depart.
But not on such sad themes, beneath thy smile

O placid Night! will memory linger long.
Pleasures, whose bare remembrance gives them
back
To be enjoyed again, rush fast and thick
Upon the expanding heart. Who doth not
mind
The moonlight rambles with the gentle maid
That won his early vow—his gaze intense
Of soft beseeching, and the blush that gave
In silent eloquence its sweet response?
Happy—thrice happy season! once enjoyed,
No counterpart e'er comes—a single spot
Of green in the wild waste of life, the past
Unclouded by the shadow of regret,
The future radiant as the glory of
The morning star.
And holy is the theme,
To which, sweet Night! thou lov'st to lead
along—
The home of childhood. But a few short years
Have sped away, since the first dawn of life,
When infancy awoke to consciousness,
And consciousness expanding, clust'ring bore
The buds that quickly opened into joys—

Joys that the home of childhood only knows—
Pure joys and ripe, that in a countless throng,
Through the young unchecked heart come
capering
After each other in a merry chase.
But why explore the regions of the past,
In search of gems to string the strand of life?
When with each little instant, ere it flies,
The bounteous hand of heaven opes for man
New channels of delight, showering down
Its gifts, alike upon the lofty and
The low. Night tunes the soul to rapturous
joy;
For here beneath this cloudless canopy,
Where all creation wears the sober garb
Of peace, the heart, its restless passions laid,
And all its warring tumults stilled, assumes
A corresponding tone, and eager drinks
The luxury of the beautiful and good.
The day may have its feverish delights,
Its train of fierce excitements and pursuits,
But when the noisy and tumultuous world
Is hushed in sleep, when the last sounds of
mirth

Have died, and thoughtless gayety sinks down
Exhausted from her giddy round, then is
The hour—the holy hour—for memory,
For meditation, and for God.

SPIRIT OF THE NIGHT WIND.

Daylight's last ray expiring,
Leaves of the real but a dream behind,
Then whither but to its own depths retiring,
Shall turn my drooping mind?

Like a dark prison seeming,
Stagnant and dull this world my soul enthralls,
That fain would go into the light that's beaming
Beyond life's stony walls.

Yet while these fancies nursing,
Still dwells the spirit in the house of clay,
And here with nature finds herself conversing,
In the old familiar way.

Thus while the still earth lying
Asleep in night's cool dew, methinks I hear
The spirit of the wind, in whispers sighing
Sweet counsel in my ear.

And thus it seems reproving:
"Why stands a mortal musing here alone?
As if the vain regrets his heart now moving,
None but himself had known.

"Over the far earth roaming,
No nook so hidden but 'tis known to me;
Now from the mountain's breezy summit coming,
Now from the booming sea.

"There's not a human dwelling—
Be it the hut where crime and want are wed,
Or gilded dome where pride's vain heart is swelling—
That I've not visited.

"Seeking, but never finding
One spot so guarded that the serpent care

Could come not in, through treacherous path-
ways winding,
To deal its venom there.

"Behind a trellis gliding,
While streamed the yellow moonlight from above,
I've heard the beatings of two hearts confiding
In their summer dream of love.

"Time, oh! how soon departing;
A twelvemonth passes, and I seek once more
That spot—the moonbeams bright as ever dart
ing
Down—down on the cold floor;

"But with love's warm flood heaving,
Why do I hear no more their hearts' full beat?
Alas! one only lives—she for her lover griev-
ing—
He in his winding-sheet.

"Morn's faint grey glimmer creeping
Through the white curtains round them closely
drawn,

I've seen upon a mother's bosom sleeping,
An infant newly born.

"Her loving eye was watching
Her treasure with a grateful, gushing joy,
Unconscious that an icy hand was touching
The forehead of her boy.

"Alas! on all sides turning,
The fatal truth is found still written there—
Each human heart has its own secret yearning,
Each has its cross to bear.

"The nun her decades telling,
In cell retired—the holy man of prayer,
The youth, his heart with mad ambition swelling,
Fame's idle wreath to wear;

"The haughty monarch reigning,
The merchant with his ships and freighted store,
The houseless wanderer his cold morsel gaining
As he begs from door to door—

"All would of joy be reaping,
But with the grain wild grass too must fall,
And sin's rank vines that round the heart come creeping—
The curse alike of all.

"Vain, then, is all repining;
The thorn still rankles wheresoe'er we roam;
Until at last life's weary weight resigning,
The wanderer finds his home."

To a sweet cadence bringing
Its song, the night wind wanders on its way,
But still the burden in my ear is ringing,
And ever seems to say,

In gentle tones reproving:
"Why stands a mortal musing here alone?
As if the vain regrets his heart now moving,
None but himself had known."

TO MISS H. McT.

Youth—magic word! that o'er the spirit brings
Those dreamy visions of departed days—
Those images of bright and lovely things—
That brief, sweet season of our smiles and tears;

Oft when the cares that in life's pathway spring,
As time rolls on and steals our years away,
Upon my brow their gloomy shadows fling,
Thou dartest to my soul a sunny ray.

And like the birds that fly from wintry wind,
O'er stormy seas to find a summer home;
My spirit leaves its present ills behind,
In fancy o'er youth's summer scenes to roam.

The bright, unclouded gayety of youth,
  The joyous sparkle of a childish eye,
Springs from the fount of purity and truth,
  And claims my heart's o'erflowing sympathy.

But most I feel, dear girl, for one like thee,
  Whose dreams of childhood tho' forever gone,
Have left thee still thy sinless purity,
  And beauty, too, and youth to call thine own.

Oft as I gaze upon thy smiling brow,
  I wish a happier fate thy days may crown,
Than 'tis the lot of mortals oft to know,
  And that thy youth may prove an endless
    one.

A NIGHT AT SEA.

Dark is the night, the fiendish winds are howling fitfully;
In inky mountains lifts itself, the hideous, hissing sea;
But fear, my heart can touch not, love! if thou but lovest me.

Still drives the storm; oh, trying hour! in bark so frail to be
Thus plunging helmless through the dark to brave a maddened sea;
But fear thee not, my precious one; no harm shall come to thee.

The timbers crack, each sail is rent, still higher leaps the sea;
Loud, and yet louder shrieks the blast in wild and mocking glee;
But high above the storm doth Heaven keep watch o'er thee and me.

Who knows! Our shattered bark may yet ride on the gale and be,
Ere breaks to-morrow's dawning light, from every danger free;
With sails all set to win the breeze—the land upon our lee.

Come closer to my heart, my love, my love that lovest me;
And if o'erwhelmed the ship goes down, we'll yet united be,
Nor fear another stormy night, through all eternity.

THE TWO WORLDS.

WHAT seems this world to me? in one bold
point
Of view, I see it as a rolling sphere,
On which I headlong plunge through trackless
space,
Like a wild courser in his mad career.

Yet all the while she seems to stand unmoved,
The centre of a fathomless domain;
Wherein sun, moon, and stars revolving seem,
Around their queen, as her attendant train.

Again she seems, in quiet majesty,
To lead the seasons of each coming year—
Stern winter—smiling, budding, blushing
spring—
Ripe summer—aumtun—all in turn appear.

I see her in her flowing robe of flowers,
Or like a brooding bird upon her nest,
'Mid foliage rich and motionless, as tranced
In noonday dreams she lies at rest.

O'er hoary forests seems she now to reign,
Dark as the shadowy brow of night; where broods
The silence of a hundred centuries,
Unbroken in those mighty solitudes.

And then she comes in evening mood, when low
The pale new moon, upon yon western hill,
Hangs like a silver lamp of transient hope,
With gleams at least of joy, lone hearts to fill.

I see her in my waking hours; in dreams
She visiteth the dreary realms of night,
To people them with forms of loveliness,
Such as the seraphs are who dwell light.

Yet oft, alas! when e'en this peerless earth
  To my bruised spirit can no balm impart,
I turn for solace to that little world,
  That hides itself within my silent heart.

For e'en 'mid ruins mouldering in decay,
  Some flower unblighted still the spot may
      bear;
And in my heart something may yet remain,
  To say to me, that all my world is there.

CONSTANCY.

'Tis man's dull way to prate that constancy
Belongeth not to aught of womankind;
That with the gentler sex, over the grave
Of one dead fancy yet another climbs,
Which in its turn lies buried with the rest.
Yet is there oft beneath the outward form
Of woman's perishable loveliness,
A soul that lifteth up its latch but once,
And letting enter but a single guest,
Closeth its gates and casts the key away.
O Love! how strong in such a soul art thou!
For with a chain of adamantine strength,
Thou girdest it around with closest ties,
That loosen not while life's warm currents flow.
O Love! how bright in such a soul art thou!
Bright as the lightning in a midnight cloud,
But flashing not like it, one moment ere
It dies: for as the sun, in torrid climes,

Ne'er suffers earth to cool, and only sinks
At night, that purest dews from heaven may
Descend, and freshen every tender plant;
Thus doth the full uprisen orb of love
Warm into life, and to perfection bring
A thousand rich, luxuriant evergreens,
That know no frost, no cold autumnal blasts;
That nourishment imbibe from bitterest tears,
And sturdier grow in sorrow's darkest hour.
O Love! how pure in such a soul art thou!
Self, with its subtile dye, discoloreth not
Thy crystal depths, transparent as the light,
Wherein are treasured aspirations pure,
And holy thoughts, and generous resolves,
Such as the angels look on and are glad.
Light but that spark, what if her passion's vain,
She still loves on—still garners in her soul
The memory of a once fond being, though
Perchance he may have proved as faithless as
The fickle wind, that sighs awhile upon
Some tender flower, then leaves it there to die;
Or he to whom confidingly she clung,
Though faithful to the last, may yet have gone
Upon the summons of an early doom.

Yet e'en this cruel blow the flame outlives,
And burns with secret fire tho' life be dead;
Or lingering on, despoiled of hope, to bring
At last a willing victim to the tomb—
The easy gate through which her soul, set free,
Rejoins its kindred essence in the skies.
  Nor is she changed when hope's fulfilled, and all
Is prosperous; the bark in which is borne
Her soul's best prize, on time's rough sea's ne'er wrecked,
Nor led by cunning wiles and smooth deceits,
Into the vortex of inconstancy;
Days, weeks, and years serve only to increase
Its precious freight of rich, delicious joy.

RHYMES ABOUT THE CABLE.

Up, up! and let's hasten away
  Through the cañon of ages to climb,
Till we sit by the fountains that play
  At the very head-waters of time.

Where chaos, cold, formless, and dead,
  In a pall of black midnight was hung,
Till creation—her smiling first-born—
  From the womb of eternity sprung.

Here on the dread confines of space,
  All silent and awe-struck we stand,
As the fair earth from nothing comes forth
  Into light at its Maker's command.

Then mark, 'mid the wonders we see,
  That in his inscrutable plan,
One hemisphere only he gives
  To be trodden by footstep of man.

The other in solitude dwells
  Far out o'er the unexplored main,
And the waters that gulf the great deep,
  He has bidden to sunder the twain.

And not until ages shall roll,
  And Adam's race multiplied be,
As the leaves of the forests of earth,
  As the sands in the drifts of the sea,

Shall the great Ocean Prophet go forth
  With faith's lofty banner unfurled,
To fathom the fearful unknown,
  And give to mankind a New World.

Where scattered broad-cast shall upspring
  The seed of the old fatherland—
Thirty million new hearts to unfold,
  And unite to the family band.

And the white sail shall swell to the wind,
  As with greetings it goes and returns:
But dull seems the breeze to the mind
  That expects, or the bosom that burns.

And what if, outwinging the wind,
  The steamers sweep over the sea?
E'en the flight of the carrier-bird
  Must too slow for this century be.

For our kindred are over the deep,
  And daily we'd wish them God-speed;
So the Cable once more must be laid,
  The Great Enterprise must succeed.

Thus the lightning is made to come down,
  And under the ocean to run;
To thrill like a delicate nerve
  Of sensation and motion in one;

Till two worlds, with an ocean between,
  Respond like the bells of a chime;
Or as two gentle lovers converse
  To the sweet beating pulses of time.

O wondrous invention of man!
  Usurping the province of thought,
That the uttermost ends of the earth
  May in closest communion be brought.

FOR ALL BUT ME.

THE cool, sweet morning air comes breathing
on me,
With store of fragrance from the world of
flowers;
I hear the quavering trill of birds beguiling,
With honied strains, the bright but fleeting
hours.
How fair and happy seems this world to be,
Alas! for all but me.

Voices I hear in various converse joining,
Beneath my window as they come and go,
And some in cheerful tones and some in laugh-
ter,
And some in tender accents, sweet and low.
Drops yet of joy there seem for all to be,
Alas! why not for me!

Hark! how the church bell in its turret swing-
ing,
Flings on the air its voice full toned and
deep,
A tranquil peace to countless bosoms bringing,
That never yet have learnt what 'tis to weep.
Full oft again 'twill ring out merrily,
But not, alas, for me!

Adown the viewless track of time I'm gliding,
And earth's rich beauties all around me
glow;
A glorious walk it seems for all abiding
In the valley we are treading here below.
But there's a land they call eternity,
Brighter, I hope, for me!

LITTLE TOMMY.

How strange to us the ways of God!
How quick is grief to grow!
And hearts without a warning word,
Their first afflictions know.

I saw a group with smiling looks,
That told the joy they felt;
Love filled the sunny atmosphere
With light wherein they dwelt.

A sweeter scene of quiet peace,
My fancy never drew—
The father and the mother, and
Those little brothers two.

Oh sudden came the mandate
From the chancery above,
To shatter, like a thunderbolt,
That shrine of life and love!

The youngest and the fairest—
  The pearl—the precious flower—
The mother's darling little pet.
  Ah, pitiful the hour!

Dropped like a blossom from a tree,
  And passed from earth away,
Yet never more to suffer
  In this vesture frail of clay.

Weep not for him, poor mother;
  'Twas thy God, who knows thy pain,
That gave him, and His blessed will
  That calls him back again.

Lift up thy drooping spirit high,
  Thy loving Lord adore,
And "Father," say, "Thy will be done,
  Now and forever more."

For precious—priceless is the grace,
  On bruised ones that's poured,
Who in their hour of darkness come
  To lean upon their Lord.

THOUGHTS OF HEAVEN.

To him who bounding not with narrow view,
His vision, to the cold, dull things of earth,
But who, with eye of faith, reaches beyond
The illusive promises of pleasure, fame,
Or power, with steadfast soul to rest upon
The thought of an eternity beyond,
There's not a gleam on the flood tide of hope,
Swimming before him, that with readier glance
His eye discerns, than that bright moment,
when,
Mortality cast off, with all its cruel stings
Of blight and sorrow, care, mistrust, and woe,
He, soul-freed as from dismal dreams shall wake;
Aye, wake to brimful joy, in greetings with
Those dear companions of his heart, from whom
He parted one by one on life's dull shore.
Glorious reunion, and so sure the bond;
Free, too, each heart, and gushing as his own.

All coldness gone; all old estrangements dead;
All grievous wounds healed up without a scar,
And every thing most prized now perfect grown.
Ah! could we but in bright, unshadowed view
This vision keep, how easy were the task,
By God imposed, to labor to the end;
Losing, in hopes of heaven, all painful sense
Of present ills, planting the pathway to
The grave with flowers, and at each step toward
That narrow house, seeing, without regret,
Another stone fall in to fill the chasm
That lies between us and eternity.

SUNDAY EVENING.

"Six days," saith the Lord, "shalt thou labor,
Six out of the seven are thine;
Six to sow, and to reap, and to gather;
But remember the seventh is mine."

He hath said it, the Lord and the Master,
But man knoweth better than He,
For he grudgeth his maker His fraction,
And frowns at His loving decree.

Oh! weary the hearts that are wasting,
And wearing their tissues away,
Because of the hard and the selfish,
Who heed not the Lord's blessed day.

So the sun t'ward the ocean is sinking,
And morning's bright hours have all gone,
Consecrated to rest and devotion,
Ere the task they have set me is done.

But at length I have crept from my prison,
  From my fetters awhile to be free,
From the din of the hive I have wandered
  To the hills that look out o'er the sea.

To these hills that rise up from the waters,
  So cold and so silent and lone,
That they seem to respond to my sadness,
  From hearts that are sad as my own.

Here I sit while the hushed hours are leaving
  Scarce even their shadows for me,
Till the great fiery globe slowly sinketh
  In the depths of the violet sea;

Till the night's wide pavilion descendeth,
  And silence sits under her pall,
And seems in the dread supernatural,
  My soul by its touch to enthrall;

Till the stars their bright radiance are darting
  From the depths of the dark dome above
As brilliant as sparkles the hoar frost,
  But cold as a home without love.

Yet steadily rest they upon me,
So pure in their passionless gaze,
That from earth and its dulness they draw me,
To God and his wonderful ways.

For He saith that the poor are His children,
As well as the mighty and grand,
That for them, too, He scatters His blessings,
As the sower the seed from his hand.

Then peace, murm'ring heart, in all bosoms
Joy mingles its measure with care;
So the rich and the poor should be brothers,
For both have their burdens to bear.

On the breeze from the bay's rippling bosom,
Comes the hum of the city again,
And as night's deep'ning shadows close round me,
I return to the dwellings of men.

EVENING HYMN.

The evening stillness sweetly steals
O'er earth and air;
The vesper chimes, in solemn peals,
The hour of prayer;
While with rapt hearts and bended knee,
We chant our evening hymn to thee,
Virgin Bless'd, to thee!

The birds with music sweet, no more
The forest fill;
The melody of day is o'er,
All, all is still;
Save that in holy harmony,
We chant our evening hymn to thee,
Virgin Bless'd to thee!

Virgin Mother, linger near,
Our prayers approve,
And upward to our Father bear
Our words of love,
While robed in faith our souls agree
To chant our evening hymn to thee,
Virgin Bless'd, to thee!

AUBURN, MY HOME.

Ah! darker still settles the gloom on my brow,
As long years creep cheerlessly on;
And sadly I turn from the dark picture now,
Of a life whose bright hopes have all gone;
For the voices that once were so sweet to my ear,
Hushed and silent forever must keep,
And the friends of my youth, to my bosom so dear,
'Neath the green sod of Auburn now sleep.

For me the bright waters of life's joyous stream
Shall glitter and sparkle no more;
Of its once cheerful sunlight there's scarce a faint gleam
Left to gladden its desolate shore.
But though the dark billows between us now roll,
And sad though my spirit must be,
Sweet solace, dear Auburn, my world-wearied soul
Still finds in its memories of thee.

DESOLATION.

Shriek, cold wind, shriek!
O'er this hill-top bleak,
Never cease with your woeful wail
Through the jagged lines
Of the tall, dark pines,
As they shake in the icy gale.

And past is the fright
Of the long, wild night,
As it lifts up its horrible pall;
And the snow and sleet,
Like a winding sheet,
Have covered the mountains all.

And the eagle swings
On his mighty wings,
And screams in the clear blue sky,
As he rushes past,
In the whirl of the blast,
To his white-hooded crag on high.

And wretched and lone
On this frozen stone,
Sits one who is longing to lie
By her side who was laid
In the grave that they made
Last night ere the storm came by.

HOPE.

Hope, like a mocking spectre, lingers last
Among the fragments of a ruined life;
And, ever and anon, drags the dark soul
Out of itself, pointing fallaciously
To images of joy ne'er to be realized.

EVA.

Eva, Eva, on thy brow,
Why that brooding shadow now?
Why that filling, swimming eye,
Quivering lip and broken sigh?
Come, my dove!
Mood like this should ne'er be thine;
Place thy little hand in mine,
Set at once thy secret free,
Give thy bosom all to me.
Wilt thou, love?

Spoke no word the pretty creature;
Sadness still touched every feature;
'Twas as clear as crystal water,
That the green-eyed ghoul had brought her
Into trouble.
Then unto my heart I drew her;
Whispered earnest words unto her;
Strove to show by soft persuasion,
'Twas a mere infatuation—
All a bubble.

Half she smiled, then through her pouting,
Half convinced, and yet half doubting.
Oh what mischief may arise
From a pair of midnight eyes!
                    If another's
Bright and blue ones should discover,
Or but fancy that her lover
Sipped a single drop of pleasure
From the jetty liquid measure
                    Of the other's.

IV.

GRANDMAMMA'S CHRISTMAS TALE.

GRANDMAMMA'S CHRISTMAS TALE.

I.

OH! we youngsters were a merry set, a keeping
Christmas night
In the parlor snug and cozy, where the fire
blazed warm and bright;
And in cushioned easy chair,
Grandmamma sat dozing there,
Quite unconscious, tho' the fun was at its height.

II.

But at length we quiet grew, then cried a rosy
little elf,
"This is stupid, let's have grandma's tale, 'tis
all about herself;
To her promise she shall keep,
So let's rouse her from her sleep;
If she's angry, why, I'll bear the blame myself."

III.

Then the saucy creature pulled the dear old
 lady's apron string,
On whose cheek was smacked a kiss that made
 the very ceiling ring,
 While she lifted up her eyes,
 With a look of half surprise,
And a smile that gentlest heart alone could bring.

IV.

In her cap of snowy dimity she looked so clean
 and neat,
Then her eye was full of kindness, and her
 voice was low and sweet;
 And the tales she used to tell,
 Wove around our hearts a spell,
In the dreary winter evenings when we'd meet.

V.

But the story of her own young life, to us was
 yet a dream,
For although we often pressed her, she con-
 trived to shun the theme;
 And the wish each day grew stronger,
 Till we vowed we'd wait no longer,
For her pledge this very night she must redeem.

VI.

Like a knot of little gypsies then we gathered
round her knees;
And our whispers fainter grew as dies the
playful summer breeze,
As in her own gentle way,
She began without delay
Her story, and the words she spoke were these:—

VII.

In my eyes sweet tears oft glisten as I sit
alone and think,
When my heart up to the gushing streams of
memory goes to drink;
And the forms of those that were
In my childhood's home so dear,
In one happy picture fancy seems to link.

VIII.

There the vine-enwoven cottage, near the elder-
clustered dell,
Stood, half hidden by the branches from the
spreading elms that fell;
And 'twere rash to disbelieve
That at morning, noon, or eve,
Holy peace about the precincts loved to dwell.

IX.

And my father, I remember him, as 'twere but
yesterday,
With his look of sweet contentedness, that al-
ways seemed to say,
Oh! how blessed is our lot,
In this quiet little cot,
From the world and all its falseness, far away.

X.

And I seem as then to watch again the fea-
tures of my mother,
As she gazed with earnest tenderness upon my
little brother;
For too frail a thing was he,
Long in this chill world to be,
While the angels waited for him in the other.

XI.

'Twas one evening, when to realms of light he
knew he must depart,
And the thought that we should lose him
nearly broke my little heart,
That he turned to me and said:
"Sister dear, when I am dead
Do not think that we shall always be apart.

XII.

"On my angel wings I'll come to thee at
evening sweet and still;
I will visit thee at morning when the sun
comes o'er the hill;
When alone, I will be near thee,
Or when loving voices cheer thee,
When in sadness, or when joys thy bosom fill."

XIII.

And that little dying brother, now an angel
pure and bright,
Said he'd bring me gentle warnings from the
fount of truth and light;
Promised always to be near
To whisper counsel in my ear,
When through frailty I might waver in the right.

XIV.

Thus my angel watched and shielded me through
each unfolding year,
Kept my heart admonished always with a salu-
tary fear;
When evil thoughts would tyrannize,
Taught my trembling soul to rise
To a purer height upon the wings of prayer.

XV.

Now the days of youth at length were o'er,
and thoughtfully I stood
On the margin where the maiden merges into
womanhood;
And a fuller joy dwelt in me,
For a fond one sought to win me,
And my virgin heart consented as he wooed.

XVI.

Ne'er give heed, my darling children, to the
voice that laughs at love,
'Tis the manna of life's wilderness that falleth
from above;
But pure hearts alone 'twill bless,
Strong in truth and earnestness,
That thro' all, and unto death, shall faithful prove.

XVII.

Oh! the earth came forth in richer garb in
those dear days, I ween;
Then, the mornings all seemed brighter, and
the evenings more serene;
Every simple flower that grew
Took a warmer, deeper hue;
Every op'ning plant put on a tend'rer green.

XVIII.

Thus I gave myself to present joy, for very
well I knew
That still nearer, each revolving sun, the hour
of trial drew;
For too oft it is the part
Of a fondly loving heart,
By long suffering to prove if it be true.

XIX.

When, alas! the day of parting came, my heart
grew chill with fear,
When I pondered all the dangers that would
soon beset my dear;
Till a voice my spirit awed,
Saying, "Put thy trust in God."
'Twas my angel that was whisp'ring in my ear.

XX.

Now a noble ship is bearing him; before the
breeze she flies.
Oh! the crowd of deep, unuttered thoughts that
in my bosom rise,
As my fancy telleth me
How she skims the Indian sea,
Skims the ocean where the spicy Ceylon lies.

XXI.

And with all my heart's devotedness I begged
of Heaven each day,
So to bless his generous efforts that he might
not long delay.
Oh! what joy then to have heard
But one only little word,
Just to tell us he was safe, though far away.

XXII.

But the weary months rolled round and yet no
tidings could we hear,
Till at last the radiant face of hope grew pale
with ghastly fear.
But my angel still would sigh:
"Trust in him who is on high,
To His true and faithful ones He's always near."

XXIII.

Then a bark from the Brazils one morn to us
the rumor bore,
That his vessel went to pieces on the Amazo-
nian shore;
And of passengers and crew,
There remained but only two,
While the rest of them were heard of nevermore.

XXIV.

But a new-born hope, as quick as thought,
sprung up within my breast,
That the one our thoughts were following
might yet survive the rest;
And I never, from that day,
Could the image put away,
Thus indelibly upon my soul impressed.

XXV.

But misfortune's crowning hour came ere many
months went by,
With the darkness of a storm-cloud rising o'er
our summer sky,
When we felt ourselves secure
In our cottage home no more;
'Twas another wound our trust in God to try.

XXVI.

By a cruel course of fraud they sought to rob
us of our own—
Of an undisputed heritage through generations
gone.
When, alas! shall righteous cause
Find its champion in the laws?
Laws in whose great name all justice should be
done.

XXVII.

Utter ruin seemed impending. In my poor old
father's face,
Deepening lines of cank'ring care from day to
day 'twas plain to trace—
From his hearth-stone to be hurled
On a cold, unfeeling world,
To begin again life's rough and toilsome race.

XXVIII.

Oh! my heart was torn by many a pang of an-
guish, thus to see
The peace that blessed those dear ones turned
to bitter poverty;
'Twas a cruel thought to brook,
So a stern resolve I took,
I would offer up myself and set them free.

XXIX.

For as he who had so crushed us was by am-
ple fortune crowned,
It was not in simple greed of gain his purpose
could be found,
For by all that art could do,
He'd sought my hand, tho' well he knew
That my heart by solemn pledge had long been
bound;

XXX.

Till I told him that his suit was vain, nay,
odious to me,
And that while the light of heaven shone his
bride I'd never be.
Then within his selfish heart
He contrived, with subtle art,
How he'd weave this web of dark iniquity.

XXXI.

Then I said, "His purpose he shall gain, but
all for their dear sake;
Of myself I have resolved a willing sacrifice to
make;"
So I dressed me on the day
In a bridal garment gay,
With a cheerful air at least my vows to take.

XXXII.

When beneath the church's hallow'd dome we
all had entered in,
And the venerable priest had arose the service
to begin,
Then these words I seemed to hear,
Like a knell upon my ear:
"Oh! to marry thus would be a dreadful sin."

XXXIII.

Then I saw no more the joyous light, nor heard
 the anthem sweet,
But it seemed as if a dark abyss were yawning
 at my feet;
 Till my angel's voice I heard,
 Like the singing of a bird;
Even now methinks the strain I could repeat.

XXXIV.

And it whispered of the vow that I had regis-
 tered above,
Of the beauty and the holiness of one undying
 love;
 Then my heart made this reply:
 "In the grave until I lie,
Ever faithful to his memory will I prove."

XXXV.

Then I spoke and said, "Dear father, there is
 naught I would not do
To shield thy age from grief or pain, or bless-
 ings to bestow;
 Peace and joy for thee to buy,
 Oh, how gladly would I die!
But you know my heart was plighted long ago.

XXXVI.

"And to wed in hate—'twere better that you
heard my funeral chime,
Than to have so dark a record placed upon
the book of time.
Though to you I know 'twill bring
Sorrow, ruin—every thing,
Yet you would not have your daughter do a crime."

XXXVII.

'Twas my father, then, that spoke, and oh!
how noble was his air,
As he turned to me and with his hands put
back my braided hair
"You are right, my child," said he,
"For this marriage shall not be;
Be the burden what it may that we must bear."

XXXVIII.

Now the one who would have bound me by a
false, unholy vow,
With a look of rage and shame upon his dark
and scowling brow,
As a deadly adder stings,
Muttered coarse, unfeeling things;
I remember how they pained me, even now.

XXXIX.

But the touch of peace was on my heart, although a pallid trace
Of the struggle I had undergone, remained upon my face.
But when the grace of Heaven,
In the blessing had been given,
And at length we turned to leave the sacred place,

XL.

Then a stranger stepped from out the crowd and took me by the hand;
Bronzed his face and thickly bearded, and his dress of foreign land;
But it proved a poor disguise,
When he cast on me his eyes,
With that look I used so well to understand.

XLI.

Then I felt a wild sensation, half of joy and half of pain,
For the shock it was so sudden it had well nigh crazed my brain.
And my heart was all a flutter;
Not a word my tongue could utter;
But my tears fell on the floor like drops of rain

XLII.

Thus 'twas in the holy presence of our blessed
Lord, that we
In the bonds of true affection should again
united be;
There he pressed me to his heart,
And I knew we ne'er should part,
For my angel stooped and whispered so to me.

XLIII.

It was Christmas morn, and never shone from
heaven a brighter day,
That our wanderer returned, and promised
never more to stray;
And 'twas on that Christmas night,
That we heard him there recite
All that happened to him since he went away.

XLIV.

He had travelled many a weary mile, and
traversed many a sea,
And the wealth that he was bringing back,
he'd gathered all for me.
In sweet peace that night I slept,
For in life I ne'er had kept
Such a holy, quiet Christmas jubilee.

XLV.

With these words it was that grandma to an end her story drew,
Then in silent reverie remained as she was wont to do.
But before the spell had flown,
That around us she had thrown,
And had left us free our pastimes to renew,

XLVI.

"'Tis a very pretty tale, that," cried a voice behind her chair;
Quick we turned, when, who but grandpa should be standing laughing there;
But 'twas plain enough to trace,
As we looked into his face,
That the old man's eye was glist'ning with a tear.

V.

NEVERMORE!

MY MARY.

Lovely in mind, in form, in face,
Thy gentle heart the dwelling place
Of every winning gift and grace,
My Mary.

Though beauty try, with witching wile,
The lazy hours to beguile,
Alas! 'tis vain without thy smile,
My Mary.

When life looks drear and sadness reigns,
And faint each hope my heart contains,
What then can ease my bosom's pains?
My Mary.

Let fate against me hurl her dart,
Let fortune, friends—let all depart,
Have I not still thy loving heart,
My Mary?

FAREWELL.

Our boat impatient bears delay,
  Hark, hark, the warning bell;
Alas! 'tis come, the fatal day,
  So Mary, fare thee well!
Farewell! dear Mary, thou shalt be,
  When I am wandering far,
To light me in my lonely way,
  A never setting star.

Our paths that part in winter drear,
  Shall meet again when spring
Shall deck the earth with grass and flowers,
  And birds begin to sing.
Farewell! though all our tender joys
  This parting turns to pain,
Old Time shall drain the bitter cup,
  And fill with joy again.

Our love again shall beam out bright,
  Though darkened now with sorrow;
In clouds though sinks the setting sun,
  He'll brightly rise to-morrow.
Soon shall we meet no more to part,
  A whispering something says,
Then here's a health to her I love,
  A health to happier days.

TO MARY.

WITH A DOUBLE WILD JASMINE.

1836.

While walking in the green wood's shade,
With thoughts of thee, my absent maid,
I spied these blossoms rare;
Upon a tender vine they hung,
Sweet, dreamy depths of moss among,
That in the soft air gently swung
Around the little pair.

In mingled sweetness round they threw
Their fragrance, for they double grew
Upon a single stem;
And thus they closely clung together
In sunny days, in chilling weather,
And each one seemed unto the other
A crowning gem.

Ah! thus, I cried, may fate decree
The current of our lives to be,
And gently onward move;
And may our hearts in joy's green spring.
Or when they're touched by sorrow's sting,
Like these sweet flowers together cling
In endless love.

LINES TO THE WILD JASMINE.
1850.

Why, little plant, so delicate and frail,
  While forest beauties all around me lie,
Wafting unheeding fragrance to the gale,
  Canst thou alone arrest my wandering eye?

Why on these golden bulbs, that tender stem,
  Do I still linger in so fond a maze?
More fondly far than on a diadem,
  Ambition's votary sets his raptured gaze.

'Tis not thy beauty, tenderness, and grace,
  That weave about me now this potent spell;
Though years ago they won for thee a place
  In my esteem, no flower could fill so well.

But thou, by skilful touch, hast joined the chain
  That links the present with the far-off past;
And one bright sunny spot in youth again
  Sweetly attracts, then binds my spirit fast.

Once on a day when soft the west wind blew,
  And my warm bosom amorous answers lent,
A double bloom of thine, of golden hue,
  I plucked and to my gentle Mary sent.

And now one boon—one other double flower,
  Which like the former I'll to Mary send;
That it may touch that happy chord once more,
  And keep it thrilling to life's latest end.

THE STEAMBOAT.

THE fires are up, the chimneys high
Roll their black volumes 'gainst the sky;
The steam set free—its deafening roar
In echoes dies along the shore.
Then at the word the line's cast off;
The 'scape-pipe puffs with hollow cough;
Our keel the parting waves obey,
And we are bounding on our way.
Then one last look we cast behind,
Some face familiar still to find,
Or yet to catch some farewell word;
But only can the hum be heard
Of mingled voices murmuring on,
Till in the distance lost and gone.
  Then turning from this fading scene,
We pace the deck with careless mien,
To gaze into the oily deep,
As through its surge we swiftly sweep;

Or watch the wreaths of vapor rise
And mingle with the misty skies—
Types of those few who from their birth—
The loveliest and the best of earth,
Are ever doomed the first to fade,
And slumber with the early dead.
  Now back and forth the engine plies,
With giant force the axle flies,
While from the fluttering wheels are thrown
Two waving tracks of milk-white foam.
Away, away! o'er the glassy tide,
Like an airy creature she seems to glide;
Aside she casts the silvery spray,
That melts beneath the waves away.
And a balmy breeze is whispering o'er
Our prow from off yon sylvan shore,
Where roses and wild jasmines bloom,
And violets yield their soft perfume.
  Here while I sit in pensive mind,
And listen to the murmuring wind,
That dimples o'er the smiling tide,
In dreams my senses seem to glide;
Fond floating visions fill my brain,
Old friends I seem to greet again;

My prattling little ones I see
Again come forth to welcome me;
And one, beloved o'er all the rest,
Weeps out her joy upon my breast.
  Oh! such sweet dreams must surely be
Faint shadows of futurity—
Promises to mortals given—
Angel whispers breathed from heaven.
Speed on my boat! like a fairy glide,
Who laughs alike at wind and tide,
O'er dancing waves, through sparkling foam,
Oh! bear me to my happy home.

SONG.

WHEN EARLY BEAMS, ETC.

When early beams of blushing morn
Are stealing through the trees;
When sparkling dew-drops deck the lawn,
And fresh the morning breeze;
When rarest beauties meet the eye,
And honeyed sweets the smell;
When on a thousand charming sounds
The ears delighted dwell:
Then from care and sadness free,
My heart in fondness turns to thee.

When list'ning to the varied songs
That fill the shady grove—
The red-breast wild, the merry lark,
The gently murmuring dove—
Or to the humming honey-bee
That sips the clover red,
Or to the streamlet gurgling o'er
Its silvery, sandy bed:
Then my spirit glad and free,
Lightly bounds away to thee.

SONG.

'TIS PLEASANT, ETC.

'Tis pleasant to watch at the eventide hour
  The sunset soft sinking away;
'Tis pleasant to gaze just after the shower
  On the rose in its dripping array;
And pleasant it is in the grove to give ear
  To the amorous plaint of the dove:
But to me, ah! 'tis pleasanter far to be near
  To the beautiful maid that I love.

The softness of twilight can never compare
  With the mildness her glances bespeak;
No rose ever scattered its sweets to the air
  That can rival the bloom on her cheek;
And the musical tones of the sorrowing dove
  Such melody never can pour,
As the accents that melt on the lips, as they
    move,
  Of the beautiful maid I adore.

SONG.

WHEN THE BRIGHT GAUDY BEAMS, ETC.

When the bright gaudy beams of the day have departed,
And silently steal the soft shadows of e'en,
When instead of the lustre the sunlight imparted,
The soft touch of twilight has purpled the scene;
We regret not that down to his rest in the ocean,
Gay Phœbus has driven his dazzling car,
But we linger to gaze with a deeper emotion
On the brightening ray of the evening star.

It is thus, my dear Moll, in the rich sunny gladness
Of pleasure I lingered enchanted a day,
And I turned from the scene with my heart filled with sadness,
When its false glare had passed like the daylight away.

But in thee, dearest girl, generous Heaven hath shown me
  A soul-soothing radiance no fortune can mar;
And oft when the light of thy smile is upon me,
  I think of that beautiful evening star.

THE NOISY OLD MILL.

1839.

How dear to my heart is the bright sunny green,
Through whose vines the white walls of my dwelling are seen;
No sounds from the world's noisy riot e'er come
To invade the sweet peace that embosoms my home.
For the soul of tranquillity breathes through the air,
And the bees' and the birds' happy music is there,
Softly murmurs the stream at the foot of the hill;
There's a charm for me e'en in the noisy old mill.

Ah! sweet 'tis, when forced from these scenes now to stray,
To fancy the eve of that too happy day,
When back to my home once returning again,
And silent and slowly I wind o'er the plain,

Come thoughts of my wife and my little ones
dear,
And the smiles of rich joy that will welcome
me there;
And oh! with what rapture my bosom will thrill
When aroused by the sound of the noisy old
mill.

1859.

It was thus in the morning of life that I sang,
'Twas a pæan of hope in my bosom that rang,
And that bright, blessed dream I so longed to
renew,
Awaited me always, sweet cottage, in you.
Where now are those mornings so dewy and
bright?
Those sweet, quiet evenings of peaceful delight?
When the clear, liquid note of the lone whip-
poor-will
Filled the woods that embosomed the noisy old
mill.

Many long, dreary years have I wandered since
then,
And joined in the strife and the struggles of men,

But my heart grows aweary, nor farther will
roam,
And fondly turns back to its sweet country
home.
Then comes a reminder all muttering and low:
"Mem'ry—nothing but mem'ry is left to thee
now
Of a form that is cold and a voice that is still:"
And I weep when I think of the noisy old mill.

SONG.

My Mary, why does fate thus sever,
  Though the weary period's short,
Hearts like ours, whose pulse must ever
  Throb in torture when apart?
For one embrace what would I give—
  One precious moment now with thee;
A lifetime in a kiss we'd live,
  Nay, nay! a whole eternity.

When earth and sky in smiles I see,
  And all around me gay and glad,
'Tis strange that though I think of thee,
  My heart should be so very sad
'Tis not that nature is less bright,
  That I no more her charms can see;
It is that naught that yields delight
  Can please unless 'tis shared with thee.

But most at night's dull, dreary hour,
  When I, alone, lie down to sleep,
Thought—busy thought—asserts her power,
  And bids me still my vigils keep.
Alone, alone, with sleepless eye,
I count the long hours tolling by,
And wrapt in tearful ecstasy,
With all my soul I think of thee.

'TIS ABSENCE PROVES.

'Tis absence proves with touchstone rare,
  If firm or frail the heart;
Pure gold a shining trace leaves there,
  No base ore can impart.

Tried thus and true, hope gently folds
  Her network round the soul,
And each frail web a fond wish holds,
  To draw it to its goal.

Thus have I sought within my breast,
  If falseness there could be,
But every fibre stands impressed
  With constancy to thee.

Like lark at morn, on upward wings
  My spirit strives to soar,
And with a loving fancy springs
  Back to its own once more.

Clear as yon star, when we're apart,
  Let faith's pure flame then burn,
Best proof how one devoted heart,
  At least, for thee doth yearn.

As mountain stream the valley seeks,
  As rivers seek the sea,
As back the wood its echo speaks,
  So bounds my heart to thee.

SONG.

THOU ART NOT HERE.

Thou art not here,
  My heart is lonely;
But as when near,
  Beats for thee only.
Ah! best beloved one,
In thine own loving tone,
When wilt thou greet me again, love;
When wilt thou greet me again, love?

Each coming morn,
  Night's gloom succeeding,
Presses the thorn
  In my heart bleeding;
Aye must its stinging pain
In this fond heart remain,
Till it is press'd against thine, love;
Till it is pressed against thine, love.

ABSENCE.

WITHOUT, all's dark and chill and bleak,
 The mournful night wind sighs;
It seems unto my heart to speak
 Of life's realities,

Of sad and lonely hours, now
 That home's sweet joys are flown;
Oh! the dull, aching void of heart,
 When one is all alone.

Yet sweetly will to-morrow's light
 Chase all this gloom away,
And to my present lonely night,
 Succeed a smiling day.

THE FIRST FIRE OF AUTUMN.

Oh, happy fireside! sweet autumnal eve!
When, from the sharp and chilly air without,
We cluster, as the dusky hour draws near,
Around the first bright blaze that warms the
hearth,
Neglected long, but cheerful once again.
There is, dear wife! a happiness complete,
Thus 'mid the prattling of our little ones
To let the time slip by; or when their joy
Is o'er, and sleep hath sent them to their couch
Of sinless dreams, to sit together by
This friendly blaze, with spirits hushed and
still,
But satisfied; nor craving aught that the
Great world, with all its pride and pomp, can on
Its votaries bestow. Ah! this indeed
Is happiness complete—a vision dim,
Of the bright joys of our celestial home.

IMPROMPTU.

Long years, dear wife, have passed away since
we,
Upon the verge of life's expanding scene,
Stood hand and hand and gazed with trustful
hearts,
Far down the dim, uncertain vale of time.
Long years, alas! and half our journey here,
Like a short morning ramble in the fields,
Already we've completed; many spots
That charmed us, have we dallied in upon
The wayside; many buds and flowers have
We culled, the passing hours to beguile.
And if some clouds have crossed our sky, soon
have
They cleared away and left all bright again.
Let us not sigh, then, at the passing thought,
That time begins to print some tell-tale marks,

Reminding us that we're no longer young.
For me—as I grow old—like others I grow
blind—
Blind to thy faults, if faults indeed are thine.
If on thy face some lines too many are
For beauty's strict requirement—if the rose
Is fainter on thy cheek, and now and then
A silvery thread steals in among thy locks
Of chesnut brown, I see them not, but o'er
The graces and the youthful charms of all
The world beside, my eyes unheeding strain
Until they rest on thee, and then I bless
My God that thou art all to me, and I
To thee.

RETURN HOME.

Oh! happy, happy, happy day!
When leaping out upon the quay,
I bid old hackey whip away,
And haste me to my Molly.

For many a weary mile I've been,
Far o'er the dark and stormy main,
But safe and sound I'm back again,
To see my darling Molly.

For when in danger, night or day,
I'd look aloft and to Him pray,
Whose voice the seas and winds obey.
He spared me for my Molly.

Whip up, my lad! for here we are,
Such hearty shouts as rend the air.
My darling little ones, I swear,
Among them, too, my Molly.

Oh! happy, happy, happy day!
Sweet sunshine round my heart doth play,
Oh! that with rapture too it may
Light up the heart of Molly.

I AM NOT OLD.

I AM not old—the count of years
  That age should reckon, are not mine.
Above me still that height appears,
  Whence downward all man's steps incline.
None of those marks as yet I bear,
  That in the aged we behold,
Nor feeble step, nor silvery hair,
  Reminds me that I'm growing old.

Yet when my senses all betray
  That o'er the earth a change has come,
That all that once was bright and gay
  Has lost its beauty and its bloom—
That Heaven my portion has decreed,
  In loneliness to walk among
Earth's joyous scenes, ah! then, indeed,
  I know that I'm no longer young.

It needs not years to steal away
  The sunshine of a happy heart;
Alas! in one brief, bitter day,
  The promises of life depart.
And what is life, when cold and dead
  Lie all the hopes to which we've clung,
And fondly nursed? Alas! indeed,
  I feel that I'm no longer young.

Oh! let Time's dreaded tide roll on
  Toward yon dim and distant strand.
Do I not see the form of one
  There beckoning to me with her hand?
Roll on, dark stream! not thus alone,
  Earth's scenes I care to dwell among;
Alas! quite old my heart has grown,
  And never more can I be young.

www.ingramcontent.com/pod-product-compliance
Lightning Source LLC
LaVergne TN
LVHW050515100826
845148LV00002B/345

* 9 7 8 1 4 2 5 5 2 1 2 4 0 *